Conscious Success

Conscious Success

The 5-Step Process To
Dissolve Stress,
Increase Productivity and
Find Your Flow at Work

By
Jacqueline Ryan Brodnitzki

Conscious Success
The 5-Step Process To Dissolve Stress,
Increase Productivity and
Find Your Flow at Work

Jacqueline Ryan Brodnitzki
Conscious Success, LLC

www.ConsciousSuccess.net

Conscious Success™ is a program taught by Conscious Success, LLC. Techniques can be learned in more depth through a Conscious Success trainer. Contact us for more information at 1-800-270-6722.

Notice:
Mention of specific companies, organizations, or authorities in this book does not imply that they endorse this book.

ISBN-13: 978-1468193145

ISBN-10: 1468193147

To my husband, Bill, who believes in my work and is always encouraging me to get it out into the world.

Table Of Contents

Conscious Success

Why Read This Book?

Life is stressful these days. In fact, there is a norm in our culture that the more rushed and hurried we are, the more important or valuable we are perceived. In a webcast I presented to the North East Human Resources Association, we polled the attending HR executives and found 75% of them think their employees are stressed, however only 25% of them offer any solution to help their employees reduce stress.

In writing this book, I interviewed 11 executives--some Human Resource professionals and some business unit heads--from small (a few hundred employees) to large (Fortune 50) organizations. See Appendix C for more information about who I interviewed and some of the interesting techniques they are using to increase engagement and performance within their companies.

Many of these executives told me health care claims are up, disability is on the rise and prescription drug usage has increased. Their employees' stress has increased consistent with rising pressure and job demands. Some signs of this stress are absenteeism, back pain, headaches, tiredness and general unhappiness. Budgets are getting squeezed and employees have to do more with less. An executive from Verizon explained, "Employees carry their responsibilities around in their pocket 24/7. A day off is never really a day off. It used to be only the executives who were always on, now even first line managers have to be on 24/7." This is true for the majority, if not all, of companies these days.

One Executive Vice President of a global insurance company told me that many of his 50 employees has cried in his office this past year. This is a company which seems to be doing it all right by offering terrific working conditions in a flat and transparent organization, in which everyone is held accountable. In addition, when pockets of organizational stress (see Appendix C for a definition of organizational stress) appear, they work quickly to remedy the situation. It seems people are having a harder time than ever managing stress.

Distraction

These executives also explained that distraction is on the rise. Employees find it harder to stay focused. They told me the number one distraction is uncertainty. Today's employees are uncertain about job security, health, family situations, personal finances, the economy, and world news. At work, employees are distracted by personal concerns and at home, employees are distracted by work. When employees come to work distracted with uncertainty, their performance and productivity suffers, their work relationships suffer, and they are discontent and unengaged. When work loads and demands increase, stress hits the roof. Employees just aren't able to handle both the uncertainty in their lives and demanding jobs without something suffering--usually their health and well-being.

The term 'presenteeism' often refers to the problems which arise from employees coming to work sick--quality suffers and others get sick. Presenteeism due to employee distraction can be just as costly to an organization. It is quite deceiving--employees may look present, but their minds are racing and they find it difficult to give their full attention to the task or conversation at hand. Performance suffers, productivity is lost and work relationships suffer. Even with many meetings and the busy nature of the work and the office space, people feel alone and disconnected from colleagues. Employees are less engaged and managers can't understand how to reengage their staff. The office feels busy, stressed and unwelcoming. Performance drops and employees look elsewhere to fill the void.

A Better Possibility

Alternatively, meet a company who decided to de-stress their employees and increase their service culture, CaLLogix, Inc.--a call center company. The CEO of Callogix, Sherry Leonard, wanted to reduce turnover and absenteeism and decided to retool the wellness program to make this happen. She added programs to help their employees reduce stress, lose weight, stop smoking and created opportunities to increase the fun and health of their office. They incorporated a number of lighthearted programs that help employees recognize each other's strengths, learn healthy alternatives to eating and enjoy coming to work. Sherry hired us to teach her employees the program you are about to learn in this book. Her healthcare provider offered weight loss and smoking cessation programs.

Within eight months the results were much more significant than Sherry could have dreamed. Absenteeism had dropped by 80%, attrition by 50%, health care claims dropped from above average to below average for their market and call escalation decreased significantly. Sherry estimates this saved the company $380,000 in the first year, about $2,000 per employee.

Through reducing distraction among her employees, Sherry is saving significant money, offering her staff a better place to work and helping them live healthier lives. She feels great about the impact she's having on her employees and about the cost savings for her company.

A Great Positive Difference

Many executives are focused on reducing their own stress and offering ways for their employees to as well. They realize the process of managing stress has huge benefits to their culture and their profitability. They can sleep better at night knowing they are supporting their employees in improving their work experience and their lives. They know their company functions better and is of better service to their customers and, very often, profits follow.

Companies who offer stress management programs and/or areas for meditation or quiet contemplation include: Google, Inc., PepsiCo, Inc., and Green Mountain Coffee (whose shares climbed 267 percent between 2004-2008).

"The stress right now is enormous; how it'll manifest has yet to be seen but I am sure there'll be a ton of burnout. Without question, this is the most important time for these types of practices."

~Herbert Benson, Associate Professor of Medicine at Harvard Medical School.

"Meditation in corporate America should maybe be more than an expression of an executive's good will or personal interest. Companies lose an estimated $300 billion annually to lowered productivity, absenteeism, health care and related costs stemming from stress, according to a study by the American Institute of Stress. Stress-related ailments account for upwards of 60 percent of all doctor visits, according to the study."

~Bill George, Professor of Management Practice at Harvard Business School and supervisory board member of Exxon Mobil Corp. and Novartis AG

Introduction

Congratulations on deciding to reduce stress in your life and be more effective personally and professionally. It is terrific that you picked up this book and are making the investment of time for yourself. Should you choose to dedicate yourself to completing the exercises within this book, the rewards are great. Not only will you reduce stress, but you will receive a new lease on life. These methods will help you to become more fully engaged in everything you do so that you enjoy your life more. You will have more energy, more enthusiasm for life and more direction.

I suggest you take a moment now to commit to yourself that you'll give this program your attention, will work through each of the five steps and will complete the exercises and homework each week.

My Story

I would like to share with you my story about how I began learning and using these techniques. I was like many of you, a hard working woman who enjoyed my work and was balancing work along with managing a household and family. I had two young boys, babies really; worked four days per week in an intense and demanding job, my husband worked long hours and I needed to find some way to reduce my stress. By chance I found a yoga class I could fit into my busy schedule. It took a lot of organization to get to this class each week. Finding babysitters and getting everyone settled before I left was a challenge. However, I rarely missed a class. It just felt too good and I knew the benefits were too important for me to stop. On one hand, I didn't want to reduce my already limited time with my children, but on the other hand I knew I needed the class for my sanity.

That yoga class was a true sanctuary for me. I could let go of all my concerns for an hour and a half and focus on myself. Each time I left I felt immensely lighter--as if a huge weight had been lifted from my shoulders and from deep inside.

I learned the power of the breath through my yoga and meditation practice in that class. While studying with different teachers, I began to read everything I could about yoga, meditation and mindfulness. I had a thirst I couldn't satisfy. Learning in this way felt nourishing to myself. Practicing each technique I learned had a deep impact on me. I eventually took a yoga teacher training and decided to leave my job to spend time with my sons and teach yoga. My husband and I worked it out--it wasn't easy losing half of our income, but it made our lives easier and less hectic. I soon began teaching yoga and meditation. More and more people came to classes on their lunch break and I was inspired by how dedicated they were to reducing their stress at lunch through yoga and meditation. They told me the yoga and meditation practice helped them be more accurate in their afternoon work, more focused and more energized. They felt that taking a break at lunch to breathe and move made them much more productive in the afternoon.

I realized many of the techniques I taught and discussed in class did not necessarily need to be practiced in the context of a yoga class. That's when Conscious Success™ was born--the program you will learn in these pages. I've taught this program at various companies including: Verizon, Cisco, Easter Seals and many smaller organizations. Many people are using these techniques daily to manage stress, be more successful in their careers and enjoy their personal lives. I love seeing the transformation people experience when they learn and practice these techniques.

I'd like to share a particularly inspiring story before we move on...

Jane's Story

Jane attended one of my programs during a very stressful time in her life. She had a high pressure job for a large telecommunications company, was raising 3 children and her marriage had recently collapsed. She felt like a complete failure. Her already high stress had hit a new crescendo.

She began practicing the techniques with earnest because they were her last hope. She had no idea what else she could do to make it through the divorce, continue to be a good mother to her children and continue to be productive and effective at work. Ten months later she joyfully told me she had made the most of this devastating experience. She began to realize that the end of the marriage was simply a change in the relationship. This new perspective helped her to negotiate with her ex-spouse so the divorce could be handled through mediation rather than spending tens of thousands of dollars on attorneys. She taught her kids that it is ok for the nature of relationships to change, and the more quickly we acknowledge change, the easier we can navigate it. She taught them resilience as she stayed focused on them and her job. She said she no longer felt like a failure, in fact, she felt victorious because she was able to handle such trauma with dignity and grace.

Not only did using these techniques get Jane through the toughest personal period of her life, they have also helped her become much more successful at work. Before coming to my program, Jane's group had been downsized from 28 people to eight. She micromanaged her staff and often her temper would get the best of her. After having an unpleasant meeting or phone call, she would chastise herself for days for her unnecessary reaction. She brought me in to work with her group because she wanted to help them reduce stress and she knew she was partially to blame for their work stress.

We found a large part of the problem was lack of communication. Her staff wasn't keeping her apprised of the status of their work, so she felt she had to micromanage. Her micromanaging distanced her staff and made them want to communicate less with her. After the team effectiveness training we conducted, her staff began communicating more effectively and Jane stopped micromanaging. Her staff began impressing both Jane and her superiors with their work and their creative ideas.

Jane is now much more steady and less reactionary. She is able to defuse angry people over the phone, rather than snapping back, and resolves issues much more quickly. She no longer has to chastise herself for flying off the handle. Instead, she is able to say, "I'm sorry, I didn't mean to react that way. Let's begin again." She is able to catch herself and resolve issues on the spot. Jane more quickly identifies when she's operating in an undesirable manner and is able to recover.

She says she can remove herself from the pressure of the situation to experience more calm and reduce her likelihood of overreacting. Her meetings go better because she stays on an even keel. She says, "As a result, I have stronger relationships with my peers and bosses." She feels people respect her much more--both her superiors and those who report to her. Since she is able to look at the bigger picture and project a clearer vision, she has more open and honest conversations with her staff.

Where Jane was once concerned with more downsizing of her group or even losing her own job, her group has maintained its size and she was promoted to head an entirely new function while retaining her previous responsibilities. Her group is now doing such a great job and is so self-motivated that rather than spending five days managing this group she now only has to devote one day per week to them while she spends the other four days managing her new function.

Jane's story demonstrates the power of the techniques you will learn in this book. These techniques have helped many people change their life for the better by reducing the impact of stress on their lives.

How To Use This Book

Each chapter contains one of five steps and offers daily homework. You will get the most out of this book if you read one step each week and practice the homework the seven days in between. The homework takes only a couple of minutes and is extremely important in receiving the maximum benefit and creating lasting change in your life. Once you have used the techniques for the five weeks in which you read this book, you will realize they offer a life-changing process for you. You will be inspired to use them through the rest of your life to continue to help you manage stress.

In Step 1, you will learn how to begin to gain control of your mind. You'll learn about the power of your mind, what happens when you get lost in thought and how to use your breath to gain control of your thoughts.

In Step 2, you will identify the limiting thought patterns that create stress and distraction in your life. Then you will learn how to dissolve these distractions and reduce your stress.

In Step 3, you'll learn how to handle any difficult situation in a productive and effective way. We will review the biggest mistakes people make in trying to reduce stress and why people start and then fail in their efforts.

In Step 4, we will change course and discuss how to make important life changes. At this point you will already have seen big changes in your life, and it will be time to commit to change going forward so you can get the most out of the rest of your life. Life is short--you can choose to waste your time or make the most of each moment. You will learn the tools to maximize your experience. You will know that you were available for your loved ones and for yourself. You won't miss the special opportunities, instead you will experience all of the moments that make life real and fulfilling. This is the key to joy and happiness. You will increase your joy and happiness by practicing these techniques.

In Step 5, you will learn the 7 habits of Conscious Success. These are the seven traits of people who are successful and who are conscious in their success. Finally, you will learn how to cement the positive change you have already made as you worked through this book. You will make a commitment to yourself for your continued growth so these techniques become a part of your life and you continue to experience growth long after you finish reading this book.

In Appendix A you will find information on how to realize even greater results through meditating.

Appendix B offers a Breathing and Meditation Practice Log to help you have greater success in keeping your practice alive. Upon finishing this book I strongly suggest you continue to practice the techniques daily. Reinforce these skills by using them every day to enrich your life.

Take time as you read this book to practice the techniques and by the time you are done, they will be habit for you. Read one step each week and practice the techniques for seven days before you begin the next step. This will help you to retain the information and ensure your ability to use the techniques for the long run.

Step 1: Harness The Power Of Your Mind

Your mind controls your experience. It is not the situations you find yourself in, but rather your mind's reaction to these situations which comprises your experience in life. I was recently at a family party and the talk turned to the weather. One person commented on how nice the breeze was while another person complained about how the heat was making her very uncomfortable. The weather was the same, it was each person's reaction to the weather which controlled their experience--making them either happy or unhappy.

Your mind consists of two parts: the conscious mind and the subconscious mind. The conscious mind is the smallest part--only about 2-4% of the whole. It is the part of the mind that creates thoughts and the part we use to figure out solutions to problems, think through situations, and ruminate over things that have happened in our lives.

The subconscious mind is much larger--about 96-98% of the whole. It is a vast open place in the mind, full of possibility, opportunity, and creative solutions. Carl Jung likened the conscious mind to a cork and the subconscious mind to the sea. He described the conscious mind as a tiny cork floating in the vast sea of the subconscious mind. Using this analogy, we typically access only 2-4% of the entire capacity of our minds.

However, when we step away from thinking about a problem, and the solution comes to us, we've accessed our subconscious mind to come up with the solution. We have quieted the thinking, conscious mind. We have accessed, or connected to, our deeper knowing.

When we use the conscious thinking part of the mind, we are often "lost in thought." We only access the knowledge that can be contained in the small cork. This conscious mind is bogged down by many thoughts and negative beliefs like worry, fear and anxiety.

I think it's fascinating that we consider the smallest percentage of our mind to be our greatest brain power. By letting this part of our mind rule our existence, worry, anxiety, and fear become our reality. In actuality it is a very tiny percent of our mental capacity and therefore not at all our reality. Our lives have so much more potential when we quiet our thinking and access our full subconscious mind. This mind is full of opportunity, creativity and possibility, which is our reality when we are not stuck in the small, limited part of our mind.

What Is Stress?

Our thoughts cause the majority of the stress we experience on a daily basis. Think back to a time when you were stuck in traffic but it did not bother you because you were listening to a good radio show or had someone fun in the car with you. Now recall a time when traffic stressed you out because you were thinking about how you were late for an appointment. The only difference between these situations was what you were thinking. In the second situation your thoughts about being late caused your stress.

The other large cause of stress is our demand and interruption-driven, fast-paced lifestyle. Dr. Roberta Lee, the coordinator of the Integrative Medicine Fellowship at Beth Israel's Continuum Center for Health and Healing in New York City and author of the *Super Stress Solution*, found a surprising fact about stress. She studied her patients who were exhibiting symptoms of anxiety, sleep disturbance, substance abuse and disengagement from their lives to find the root cause of these symptoms. Because the symptoms were typical of post-traumatic stress disorder she had assumed they came from one traumatic event, however she found the symptoms did not stem from a single event. Instead, these patients had been living under such extreme stress for so long they didn't even know they were stressed. The stress had simply become part of the landscape of their lives.

Stress levels have increased over the past 10 to 20 years, to a point where our typical stress is what would have been considered extreme stress 10 or 20 years ago. We are now dealing with elevated stress every day and we consider this stress to be part of normal life. Because we're barraged all day long with demands, decisions and interruptions through email, cell phones and the internet, our body and our nervous system is on high alert at all times. Our nervous system is anticipating problems all day long. Do you notice you can't stop checking your e-mail? Are you always looking something up online or checking for messages?

This state of high alert is our fight or flight response. With this response engaged we react much more quickly and much more strongly to anything out of the ordinary. Have you ever had a day where it feels like everything is going wrong? A minor thing happens, like you spill coffee or tea on your pants, and it sends you into an uproar; you start slamming things and your morning is ruined. You know deep down that what just happened is a very minor incident, but because your stress is already heightened, that one minor incident throws self control out the window.

Lost in Thought

I refer to being 'lost in thought' when you are completely caught up in your thoughts. For example, when you are walking and you are thinking about a situation that happened the day before. Because you are thinking about something that happened at a different time, you are not experiencing your walk. Rather, you are re-experiencing that meeting or conversation you previously had. The walking doesn't register in your consciousness, instead, you picture and feel the emotions of that meeting. You may even finish your walk and not have seen any of your surroundings.

Thinking about future events works the same way. How many times have you driven to work and did not notice the drive because you were thinking about your day to come? Perhaps you drove for a half hour and you do not recall much of your drive. How many times have you been on the phone and missed part of the other person's explanation or you have been in a meeting and missed a portion of the discussion?

It is easy to notice when someone else is lost in thought. I'm sure you can recall many instances when you were on the phone and can tell the other person is reading e-mail because they don't respond in their typical way. Or you can see in someone's eyes they are thinking about something else while you are speaking with them. Being 'lost in thought' diminishes your effectiveness in interacting with others and making decisions. The other person feels as if they aren't important to you because you are not listening fully to them. While being 'lost in thought' may be a cultural norm these days as everyone checks their phones constantly, it still sends a negative message to the other person.

Try This: Lost In Thought Exercise

Take a moment to write about a recent instance in which you were lost in thought. Here is an example: I was 'lost in thought' as I was speaking with my boss. I was thinking about how I would respond to her accusation and did not hear some things she said. I jumped in with excuses for my team and did not realize she had already heard about how my team responded. She got angry and I lost credibility with her. Had I been present for our conversation I would have understood what she knew about the situation and responded with the information she needed rather than being defensive. I would have proven, rather than lost, my credibility.

Now, let's write this out in a few steps:

First, describe what you were doing recently when you were "lost in thought."

Recently I was 'lost in thought' as I was:

_____

_____

_____

Write what you were thinking about as you were lost in thought--was it something in the past or something in the future?

I was thinking about:

_____

_____

_____

_____

_____

_____

_____

Note how being lost in thought affected the situation. For instance, being lost in thought during a phone conversation caused you to have to ask the person to repeat what they were saying.

Being lost in thought affected the situation by:

_____

_____

_____

_____

_____

How would the outcome have been different if you had been present for the situation? Perhaps you lost some credibility or trust by having to ask the person to repeat what he or she said. Perhaps the person was telling you something very important and you missed an important detail related to a project. Perhaps you missed an important business opportunity.

If I had been 'present' for the situation, the outcome could have been different in this way:

_____

_____

_____

_____

_____

_____

_____

_____

The point is, we can never get back a moment once it's gone. Each moment is important. Every time we think about the past or the present, we miss the current moment. When we train our minds to stay in the present moment, we are more effective in our work and our relationships and life is more full and enjoyable.

Your Breath

One powerful and easy way to help yourself decrease stress is through breathing deeply. Your breath controls your nervous system; a deep breath instantly calms your nerves. A shallow breath tells the nervous system to be on the look out for danger, and creates the stress-response in the body.

Dr. Andrew Weil, the founder and program director of the University of Arizona Center for Integrative Medicine, is a huge proponent of breath and the health effects of taking deep breaths. He says, "One of the most important tools you can incorporate into your life to affect the quality of your life, is a deeper slower breathing practice. Breathing exercises are a wonderful way to reduce anxiety, agitation and stress, while promoting relaxation, calm and inner peace. Breathing strongly influences physiology and thought processes, including moods." Because your breath controls your nervous system, your breath is the key to reducing tension and stress.

Most people breathe using only the top third of their lungs. This shallow breathing creates a fight-or-flight response in the nervous system. When you breathe this way, you are instructing your nervous system to be on guard for the next danger or the next emergency. Notice how you are breathing right now. Are you only filling your upper chest with breath? If so, you're only using the top third of your lungs and your nervous system is on high alert--your stress response is kicked in to high gear.

Shallow breathing also affects the quality of your voice and your credibility. I attended a seminar in which a woman who owned two successful companies gave a presentation. She had a chance to comment during the MC's introduction and she sounded quite confident. However, once she took the stage in front of the audience, her breath became shallow and quick. Her voice became high-pitched and she sounded nervous. I had a hard time hearing her message because of her nervous demeanor. If she had simply slowed down and breathed more deeply her message would have come across a lot stronger and she would have appeared more confident and in control.

Breathing through your nose automatically makes your breath deeper and calms your nervous system. Inhaling while extending your belly forward, brings oxygen into the lowest area of your lungs. Exhaling, by pulling your belly back to your spine, removes stale air from your lungs. Breathing in this way, you use the diaphragm to pull air in and out of your lungs more efficiently while calming your nervous system.

Within 17 seconds of taking a deep breath, you send increased oxygen throughout your body. As you breathe, the deep breath brings more oxygen into your bloodstream and this oxygen is pumped throughout your body immediately by your heart. Your brain, organs and cells function better and are healthier when they receive this increased oxygen.

Try This: Deep Breathing Exercise

Place your hands on the lowest part of your abdomen and sit up straight so your back is not against the back of your chair. Let your spine be very tall. Take a deep breath in through your nose and as you breathe in, extend your belly forward. As you breathe out through your nose, let your belly retreat back towards your spine.

As you breathe in again extend your belly forward, and as you breathe out let your belly come back towards your spine. Continue to breathe in and out like this. With each breath let your belly expand even more and with each exhalation let your belly come back closer to your spine to let all of the breath out of your body.

As you continue breathing in, imagine your abdomen is extending in all directions. Forward and back, side to side, top to bottom. Then, let the breath fill your chest, expanding your lungs and ribs in all directions. Notice how good it feels to expand your lungs and your ribs. Continue with ten deep breaths this way.

Many people have difficulty expanding their belly on the inhalation. If this is your case, be patient with yourself and keep trying. Place your hand on your belly as you breathe in to feel it expand. You should find you are able to breathe this way within a week or two with daily practice. Babies breathe this way automatically, but I've noticed somewhere around 3rd or 4th grade, many children reverse the action of their belly as they breathe in. Keep practicing and you will soon be able to expand your belly on your inhalation.

By focusing on deep breathing you immediately bring your mind to the present moment. Whenever your mind wanders--to what you are going to have for your next meal, what happened this morning or what will happen tonight--you are caught up in your thinking mind. You are 'lost in thought' and missing the present moment.

When you breathe deeply and feel your breath completely, you remain more even. It is hard to be as afraid, anxious, worried, angry, or sad when breathing deeply. These emotions are only thoughts. When, you experience the present moment, the power of the emotion diminishes. You are able to respond clearly rather than being needlessly provoked by your emotions. You can significantly reduce negative thoughts which cause stress by breathing deeply throughout the day. To manage a stressful situation, take three deep breaths and imagine stress leaving your body. Once the stress is reduced you can act most effectively for the situation.

Becoming Present

Let's go back for a moment to the discussion about the subconscious part of the mind. This part of the mind--about 96 to 98 percent--is completely open to possibility, is creative, has wonderful ideas, and wonderful solutions. When you are lost in thought, you are only using 2 to 4 percent of the mind--you are limited to that small cork. When you focus on your breath, you are in the present moment and are accessing that 96 to 98 percent of your brain which opens you to your unlimited potential.

A wonderful way to experience this, and something that I do often, is to go for a walk in the woods, at the beach, in a park or somewhere outside where you can experience nature. When you are walking outside observe everything around you. Breathe deeply. This is when you will receive inspiration, ideas and access your vast intelligence.

For example, before writing this section I went for a walk in the woods. During my walk, instead of thinking about how I would write this chapter or whether the information is valuable or interesting, I simply walked and looked at everything around me. The structure of this chapter became clear to me toward the end of the walk because my mind was open.

You also have access to the subconscious mind whenever you are in the present moment--even when you are working. When you are concentrating on your work and focused on what you are doing in the present moment, you create your best work.

Have you ever noticed that you get your greatest ideas in the shower, walking outside or when you are working on a hobby? When you are fully engaged in these activities you are often able to be in the present moment and access the subconscious part of your mind. Rather than being caught up in your limited, conscious part of your brain, you're in the flow, doing what you love. Your greatest ideas arise when you are in your flow. A great way to access your flow is by feeding your soul. When you do something you love, you are fully engaged, present and open to possibility.

Try This - Feed Your Soul

Do something that feeds your soul and allows your mind to be open and aware every day. It could be a hobby, gardening, or walking in the woods. Perhaps going for a run, walking on the beach, or playing with your pet. It may be playing with your kids or grandchildren, doing yoga, meditation, tai chi or chi gong. Simply do something each day that feeds your soul.

By doing something like this each day you can set the scene to receive inspiration, ideas and feel creative. Take a moment to commit to this right here. I plan to feed my soul each day by doing one of the following ten activities:

1._____

2._____

3._____

4._____

5._____

6._____

7._____

8._____

9._____

10._____

Now it is up to you to do this. This practice will relieve your body of stress. It will clear up and clean out your mind, and it will help you access your deeper wisdom and creativity.

When I worked with a Director and her team, of a Fortune 100 Computer Networking Company, I was surprised by how adamantly she advised her team to schedule 30 minutes on their calendar each day to feed their soul. She knows how important this simple step is to keeping her team members feeling good and performing at their peak levels.

Step 1 Homework

This week you will practice becoming present through breathing and doing something each day that feeds your soul.

1. Take 10 deep breaths each morning upon waking. Find a comfortable place to sit. Sit up nice and tall and fill your belly as you inhale and let your abdomen relax back to your spine as you exhale.

2. Take 10 deep breaths each night when you get into bed. It's perfectly all right if you fall asleep before you get to the tenth breath.

3. Do something that feeds your soul each day. Schedule 30 minutes on your calendar to make it a priority.

Place a ✓ for each day you practiced breathing:

Day 1	Day 2	Day 3	Day 4	Day 5	Day 6	Day 7

What did you notice this week?

Step 2: Identify and Dissolve Limiting Thought Patterns

Most peoples' minds are constantly busy. After all, it is the brain's job to think. We saw in the last step that when we are thinking about something other than what we are currently doing, we are not in the present moment. Therefore, it is important to gain control over our minds to bring ourselves back to the present moment. It **is** possible to control your mind.

Thought Patterns

In Step 1 we learned how our thoughts cause stress. In this chapter we will talk about how to identify your own specific thought patterns that cause your stress. There are 12 typical thought patterns on which most people focus. In any given week, people tend to have three or four thought patterns running through their minds. Read through the chart below and descriptions beginning on the next page. Notice which 3-4 thought patterns resonate for you.

Annoyance	Worrying	Rehashing
Judgement	Comparing	Planning
Resentment	Fear	Anger
Anticipating	Regretting	Sadness

Thought Pattern Descriptions

- Annoyance: Do you find yourself easily annoyed about little things? Do they grate on your nerves?

- Judgment: Are you quick to judge? Do you judge how someone is acting, the kind of car someone is driving, or how someone is managing life?

- Resentment: Do you find yourself thinking about and resenting things that have happened in the past or things that other people have done to you?

- Worrying: Are you worrying about things that will happen in the future or the ramifications of things that have happened in the past? Do you worry about yourself, your children or other family members? Do you worry about the world and current events?

- Comparing: It is very common to compare ourselves to others every time we enter a new situation. Perhaps you focus on something the other person does that you do better or worse. Usually when comparing, we never measure up to our own expectations or to the other person. We always compare our insides to someone else's well put-together facade. This often makes us feel inferior. We forget that everyone is vulnerable on the inside.

- Fear: Are you afraid of things that may happen in the future? Are you anxious? Anxiety often begins with fear.

- Rehashing: Do you play conversations over and over in your mind? Perhaps you keep thinking about something you did that you wished you had not done.

- Planning: Do you find yourself thinking about the future a lot? Planning what you're going to do this afternoon, tonight, next week or the next vacation you're going to take? This is a big one for me. I'm a planner and I catch myself planning future events while I miss what is going on right in front of me. When I do this I know I need to bring my focus back to what I am doing.

- Anger: Are you quick to anger? Sometimes we go through periods of being more quick to anger. Is this a particularly timely item for you right now? Are you quick to anger about that person who cut you off in traffic or about someone who was rude to you?

- Anticipating: Do you often try to think of the next thing that will happen? Anticipating is not necessarily planning, it's more thinking about what could happen. For example, "If I run into her today, how am I going to respond?" Or, "When that issue comes up in that meeting, what am I going to say?" Or, "This person usually makes some comment about xyz whenever I see him and it really drives me nuts! How am I going to react when it happens today?"

- Regretting: Do you find yourself feeling bad about things you've done in the past?

- Sadness: Is there something that makes you feel sad? Do you often find your mind lingering on sad things that have happened in your life or that you see in the news?

These 12 thought patterns typically play over and over in peoples' minds each day. Our brain thinks it is its job to focus on these thoughts. Having an understanding about which thought patterns you are experiencing right now is important knowledge. Each time you notice your thought patterns arising more frequently, it is an indicator that you are experiencing more stress. It is helpful to view your own thought patterns as a barometer of your current stress level. Once you have this understanding you can use techniques to control your stress before it sky rockets out of control.

Perhaps you have already noticed these patterns and have been working to quiet some of these thoughts. Each person has many levels of these patterns and it usually takes time to reduce their grip. You can view challenging situations, which will encourage these thought patterns to arise, as opportunities to diminish the strength of these thoughts.

There are times when thought patterns, such as planning or rehashing, can serve us well. They are effective when deliberately setting aside time to focus on goal setting or learning from past situations. Do everything deliberately. Don't become hijacked by thoughts of planning or rehashing. Being hijacked by thoughts is disruptive when you are trying to understand a customer's perspective or when you are speaking with a co-worker. Instead, be fully present with that person. Do not plan the rest of your day or another project. When you are with a loved one, be fully present with that person. Do not waste the opportunity by planning some other event.

Sometimes we plan just because it's a habit and we find ourselves planning even the mundane aspects of life that do not require planning--like our morning routine. How many times have you laid in bed planning out your morning? There are many things we do during the day that we don't have to think about in advance, and without planning we can do them just fine. We do not have to clutter our brains thinking about them.

We have become conditioned to think about everything we do. However, when we think less and instead notice what is around us, our intuition, gut or inner wisdom are activated more strongly and we make better decisions and do things better. That is why often our best solutions come to us in the shower, when we're walking or running, in the middle of the night or upon waking. When we are not busy thinking, our mind can relax and our best creative ideas have an opportunity to come forth.

Negative Effects of Thought Patterns

The constant replaying of thoughts has six significant negative effects on your life:

1. **Decreased effectiveness in communication--** when you are caught up in a thought, you are much less tuned in to the other person. You respond to your own thoughts rather than what the other person is saying. As a result, you often do not respond in the most helpful way for the situation. For example, a woman told me about how her communication has improved with her son since she has stopped anticipating as much. He is home alone each day while she is at work and he has been getting into trouble. During her drive home after work she used to anticipate the trouble he had gotten into. As a result, when she walked in the door, she would order him around and yell at him. Once she began using her drive home to breathe deeply, she found she could respond to her son in a much better way when she arrived home.

2. **Decreased effectiveness of work--**if you are sitting at your desk working on a project but thinking about a meeting you had last week, you're not going to be as creative, you may overlook important aspects of the project, and there is a high risk that you will make mistakes.

3. **Decreased understanding of a situation--** when you are caught up in your own fear, anger or anxiety, you're not catching the subtleties of the situation and you're less perceptive. It is very easy to get caught up this way and to think that your own perspective is the only way to look at a situation. However, this decreases your ability to

understand the entire situation and respond appropriately.

4. **Decreased productivity**--any time spent thinking about something other than what you are currently doing is time away from the task on hand. It is wasted time which leads to decreased productivity.

5. **Increase in sadness, anger and fear**--as thoughts come up, you experience the situation that made you sad, angry or fearful. You experience the strong emotions as they course through your body. The brain does not realize that you are just thinking, rather you experience the situation, your heart beat races and your nervous system becomes agitated. You relive the past experience or preview the future situation.

6. **Increased unhappiness**--most of our thoughts are negative. Research shows that 80-90% of our thoughts are negative. Think about your own thoughts, how often are they pleasurable? I bet most of the time you are beating yourself up for something you said, angry at someone else for something they said or did, or anticipating a difficult conversation. When we have negative thoughts running through our minds we feel unhappy. This is the opposite of how we want to feel. In Marci Shimoff's book, *Happy For No Reason*, people polled around the world say the number one thing they want is to be happy. However, 80-90% of our thoughts reduce our happiness. If we want to be happy, why do we let unhappy thoughts rule our lives?

There is a Buddhist proverb that says, "Pain is inevitable, suffering is optional."

Painful things may happen in our lives, however the suffering we create with our thoughts is optional. We can end our suffering by managing our thoughts.

Try This: Negative Thought Pattern Exercise

This is a very valuable exercise and takes about 15 minutes to complete--you'll figure out which thought patterns are necessary for you to dissolve.

Step 1: In the left column of this chart (it continues on the next two pages), write the three or four thought patterns (from the chart on the first page of this chapter) that resonate with you. Choose the thoughts you've experienced most over the past week. Write each thought pattern in one of each of the left boxes in the first column.

Step 2: There is usually a situation that brings up a thought pattern. What are the top three likely situations that bring up your thought patterns? Write them in the center box next to each thought pattern.

Step 3: In the third column write the effect of the thought pattern on each of the three likely situations that bring it up.

Thought Pattern	Likely Situations	Effect on Each Situation
1	1.	1.
	2.	2.
	3.	3.

Thought Pattern	Likely Situations	Effect on Each Situation
2	1. 2. 3.	1. 2. 3.
3	1. 2. 3.	1. 2. 3.

Thought Pattern	Likely Situations	Effect on Each Situation
4	1. 2. 3.	1. 2. 3.

Here is an example:

Thought Pattern	Likely Situations	Effect on Each Situation
1. Anger	1. News 2. Being cut off in traffic 3. Someone is rude to me at work	1. I am short tempered at home 2. I drive aggressively 3. I avoid her and am rude. I don't listen to her. We never get the problem resolved. She might have good ideas, but I wouldn't know. Our hostility affects meetings and people hate it.

In a slightly different scenario, imagine the likely scenario for anger is seeing someone who has been rude to you in the past. How do you respond when you see that person walking toward you? Most likely you bristle, put up your defenses and get ready to attack at the slightest provocation. How does this affect your interaction? Is it a given that this person is always going to be rude? Could this person's rude behavior stem from them anticipating your defenses? Do you miss an opportunity to hear a different perspective, learn something valuable and perhaps even cultivate a better relationship with this person?

Use this Negative Thought Pattern chart as a barometer for understanding your stress levels. When you notice your thought patterns being triggered more frequently, you know you are under more stress. This is an opportunity to take some deep breaths to stop the thoughts from creating a full blown story and taking over your experience.

What is fascinating about this exercise is you begin to see how your thought patterns affect virtually every situation in your life. Every situation is neutral, your thoughts and subsequent response are what make it "good" or "bad." For example, someone cuts you off--they're not doing it to be mean to you, they just realized they're in the wrong lane and they have to make a turn. Yet, your anger about being cut off makes you flip out and start screaming at the person. What is the effect on this situation? Your blood pressure rises, your heart beats faster. Maybe it feels good to yell at first, but then your throat hurts and your heart is racing. It would probably have been better to remain calm than to risk heart attack.

Recently I was with some friends and one of them made a comment that felt like an attack on my mothering style. I could feel myself becoming angry, but I chose to breathe deeply rather than respond. I later realized that my friend was simply saying that she would not be a good mother to boys and she was not attacking my style. I was really glad I had not reacted based on my earlier angry thoughts.

We are often so caught up in our own responses to situations that we automatically assume our relationships will remain the same. We often think, "Well, this person is just this way." Because of this we stop listening to them and hearing what they truly have to say. We miss valuable opportunities. What if the person didn't even intend to be rude and it was you who interpreted the comment that way?

Typical Reactions To Stress

The following chart shows the typical reaction to stress. This concept is described by Daniel Goleman in his book, *Emotional Intelligence*. The vertical axis represents the intensity of emotion and the horizontal axis represents elapsed time. When something stressful happens, our emotions shoot way up in intensity (represented by the line with triangles). Our brain is caught up in the emotion, the fight-or-flight response kicks in, and we experience clouded, non-rational thinking.

Think about the last time you were really angry at someone who cut you off in traffic. Maybe you were even so angry that you flipped them off and thought about hitting them with your car...not too rational.

Eventually the emotion begins to decrease and rational thinking returns. This is represented by where the emotion line intersects with the rational thought line (the line with squares on it).

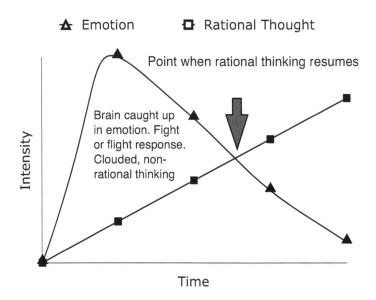

This chart shows what happens when you use stress-reduction techniques such as deep breathing to manage stress.

Rational Thinking Resumes More Quickly When Stress Reduction Techniques Are Employed

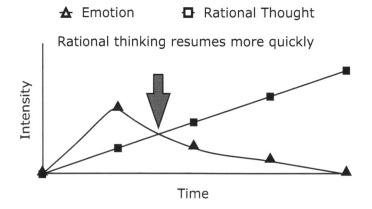

The intensity of emotion is reduced considerably, there is less of a fight-or-flight response and rational thought resumes much more quickly.

Emotional and Social Intelligence

One of the most beneficial outcomes people experience when doing these exercises and practicing the stress reduction techniques is an increase in emotional and social intelligence. A huge body of research has been created about the important role of emotional and social intelligence in strong employee performance and personal effectiveness over the past 20 years.

It has been shown that a very high IQ alone does not guarantee successful job performance. Both emotional and social intelligence are necessary for optimizing performance on the job and in cultivating relationships.

Bill George is a huge proponent of mindfulness techniques (the types of techniques in this book). He also feels emotional intelligence is critical to success. He wrote in his blog, "Gaining awareness of oneself – our motivations, our destructive emotions, our crucibles, and our failings – is essential to being an effective leader. Based on my research into leaders, I have found the greatest cause of leadership failures is the lack of emotional intelligence and self-awareness on the part of leaders. I cannot name a single high-level leader who failed due to lack of IQ, but am aware of hundreds of leaders that have been unsuccessful due to their lack of emotional intelligence (EQ). The destruction of organizations caused by their shortcomings is staggering."

He goes on to say, "Having observed hundreds of leaders under pressure, I have no doubt that self-awareness and self-compassion are the essential aspects of effective leaders, especially when they are under stress and pressure. Leaders who develop and maintain these qualities are better able to lead others mindfully and to empower people to perform at a very high level. With a shared sense of purpose and common values, organizations can then take on very challenging goals and overcome great difficulties and achieve outstanding results on a sustainable basis."

Emotional and social intelligence (EI) greatly increases the ability to work well with others and to control stress. Many people find that as they develop EI through breathing practices they do better in their jobs, more opportunities open up to them, and their work is more creative and of a higher quality. They also notice big rewards in their personal life with stronger relationships with friends and loved ones, more positive encounters and more ease in life.

Emotional and social intelligence begins with **self-awareness** and noticing your thoughts. Once you are able to notice your thoughts, you have better **self-management**--the ability to manage your thoughts, not let your emotions take over, and self-motivate. **Social-awareness**, the ability to be aware of other people, understand how they function, and know how best to work with them is the third piece to the puzzle. It all comes together in **relationship-management**--how we relate to others, work in teams and inspire others.

Developing these skills begins with the work we have done in this chapter to be self aware enough to notice when we are hijacked by thoughts. Ask yourself, what are the thoughts that are preventing me from living my best life, doing my most effective work, engaging in healthy relationships, and enjoying each day?

Dissolving Limiting Thought Patterns

Now let's practice some techniques to bring you to the present moment and reduce stress. As a result, you will notice greater happiness and joy in your life. These techniques immediately calm the nervous system, thereby calming your body and mind. As you practice these techniques your emotional and social intelligence automatically increases. Let's begin by reviewing and practicing the Deep Breathing Exercise again.

Try This: Deep Breathing Exercise

Take a moment to come back to the present moment with ten deep breaths. Sit up tall, turn away from distractions and take ten breaths to rejuvenate yourself for the rest of the day. Breathe in through your nose filling your belly deeply. Breathe out letting the breath be released completely through your nose. Breathing in let your belly expand in all directions and breathing out let your breath flow out easily.

With your third breath, bring even more air into the body filling your belly then lungs. Take seven more breaths. Make sure you are bringing in as much breath as you can. As you breathe out, let all of your breath out of your body as you pull your belly back to your spine. Take this time for yourself, knowing that the amount of time you spend taking ten deep breaths, is going to come back to you tenfold in your health, your productivity and your effectiveness.

Hopefully you have been doing this Deep Breathing practice each morning upon waking and each night as you lie in bed. Many people tell me that it helps them to sleep better. If they tend to have trouble going to sleep, they go to sleep easier. If they tend to wake during the night, they get back to sleep more quickly and sleep through the night more consistently.

Try This: Fountain Breath Exercise

This is a terrific exercise to use if you are feeling emotional or have been around someone who was negative. This is a great tool for clearing up any tension in your body.

Sit with your back straight and close your eyes. Begin by breathing in and imagine that a fountain is rising up through the center of your body to a point above your head. As you exhale, imagine the water coming down all around your body relaxing the muscles of your neck, chest and back, and clearing out any negativity from the air around your body.

With each breath the water comes up through your body, removing any negative energy and thoughts and as the water cascades around you, it clears your mind and cleans the air. Take eight more breaths like this, breathing in, imagining the water cleaning out your insides--getting rid of the sludge and other things that no longer need to be inside. As you exhale, imagine the water relaxing your muscles and cleansing your skin and the air around you.

When you are done, slowly open your eyes and notice how you feel.

Many people find Fountain Breath to be quite powerful. I have received many comments about how this technique reduces all sorts of intense emotions.

Try This: Exhaling Through The Mouth Exercise

Another technique which is particularly beneficial in a stressful situation is breathing in through your nose and out through your mouth. This breath instantly calms your nervous system and helps you practice letting go of the stress you just encountered. If you are experiencing some particularly negative or stressful thoughts, this helps you let them go. Imagine that each thought you have during the day is a piece of luggage. Visualize yourself dragging around a day's worth of luggage. Pretty heavy huh? Now, try this breathing technique.

Breathe in through your nose while lengthening your spine. Breathe out through your mouth audibly or even with a sigh as you relax your neck, shoulders and back muscles while keeping your spine straight. Take 4 more deep breaths and with each exhalation imagine you are letting all of the tension out of your body. Imagine you are setting down the heavy luggage you have accumulated during the day.

Do you feel lighter and more relaxed? How much more enjoyable and better can you live without having to carry that luggage?

Now let's move on to a technique called noticing. Noticing is particularly helpful when you find you are lost in thought. Let's say you are in a meeting, on a call, or face to face with someone and you realize you are thinking about lunch, the next thing you have to get done, or about how you wish this person would just stop talking. Perhaps the other person is talking so much because you are not listening. Just by giving someone your full attention, you may find they become more succinct or you are better able to direct the conversation to keep it relevant.

This technique will bring you back to the conversation and help you respond more effectively. You will be more perceptive and have a better understanding of the situation.

Try This: Noticing Exercise

When you realize you are thinking about something other than the conversation or meeting in which you are participating, begin to notice something that is right in front of you. Notice the person's eyes with whom you're speaking, notice their glasses, hair or earrings. If you're in a meeting or on the phone, notice the plant, mug or phone that is in front of you. Notice everything you can without judging what you see. Take the time to look very closely and notice something you've never noticed before.

When you are outside walking or driving in your car, rather than getting lost in thought, notice as much of your surroundings as you can. You will be more alert and you will enjoy your experience more.

Step 2 Homework

Your homework this week will help you gain control over your thoughts. The only way to gain control is to work at it every day, so it is critical to spend a couple minutes doing your homework each day. It will be time well spent.

1. At the end of each day, identify a thought pattern that arose, what situation provoked it, and how you were able to dissolve it. What was the outcome of noticing your thought pattern and dissolving it? Use the chart (which has a row for each of the next seven days) on the next page to record your experience.

2. Continue to practice ten deep breaths each morning and each evening before bed. Record your practice on the next page.

3. When anything comes up during the day that is stressful, or if you notice you are angry, sad, or anxious, take three to ten deep breaths right in that moment. No one will even know you are doing this. Just breathe in and out a few times through your nose and then respond to the situation. Others will think you are listening to them closely and giving them a thoughtful response. You will be more calm and the other person will feel this. Your response will be much clearer, more effective, and more creative.

Homework - Step 2

Thought Pattern	Situation That Brought It Up	How You Dissolved Thought Pattern	Outcome

Place a ✓ for each day you practiced breathing:

Day 1	Day 2	Day 3	Day 4	Day 5	Day 6	Day 7

What did you notice this week?

Step 3: Handle Difficult Situations Effectively

During one of our programs a female participant exclaimed, "There are no negative situations, only negative reactions!" Nothing could be more true. If you think about anything that has happened in your life, the decision about whether it is good or bad is based upon the label you gave it and your resulting reaction.

Let's think about a situation that most people would agree is horrible like getting laid off. Most people I know who have gotten laid off would say, after the fact, that it was actually a gift. It was either a wake-up call to make a change, modify some habits or it gave them an opportunity to find a better or more interesting job. People I know who have gone through a divorce have been freed up to get to know themselves better, realize what they truly want in a partnership and some have found someone who is a much better match for them.

We are quick to react negatively to most things that happen to us. Next time you notice a negative thought or reaction forming, see whether you can breathe with it and notice even one small gift in the situation. It might take you a while to find the gift. Give yourself time to look for it. I heard a minister once say that we should not let go of any pain until we find the gift it has given us. I would include that it is important to breathe as we experience the pain which allows us to reduce the intensity of the pain and see the gift more clearly.

When facing difficult situations I suggest two separate processes. The first is, **STOP** and the second is **The ABCs For Handling Any Situation Effectively**. Both of these help turn difficult situations into productive learning experiences. These processes allow you to manage situations in a way that keeps stress levels low and ensures your best response to the situation.

STOP

The first process, **STOP,** is adapted from Elisha Goldstein, Ph.D.'s article, *"Stress got you down? Try this tip to balance throughout the day."*

When Faced with a Difficult Situation... STOP

Stop what you are doing

- Don't respond, say or do anything.
- Put your work down.

Take a breath

- Breathe normally and naturally and feel your breath coming in and of your nose.
- Say to yourself silently, "in" as you are breathing in and "out" as you're breathing out to help you focus on your breath.

Observe your thoughts, feelings, and emotions

- Notice any thoughts and emotions, and name them (for example, anger or resentment).
- Remember that thoughts are not facts and are not permanent.
- Research out of UCLA says that just naming your emotions can have a calming effect.
- Notice your body. How is your posture? How do you feel on the inside?

Proceed in a more calm and in-control state

- Continue your conversation noticing everything you can about the other person and listening to them fully.
- Go back to your work and look at it with fresh eyes.
- Do something that will support you in the moment (for example, take a walk, stand up, stretch).

ABCs to Handle Any Situation Effectively

Many of the steps in this next process were taught to me by one of my teachers, Pema Chodron, an American Buddhist Nun.

ABCs to Handle Any Situation Effectively

Awaken Your Awareness of Stress

Breathe 3 Times and Focus

Call on Compassion

Don't Bite the Hook

Eliminate Your Story

Find Friendship and Gentleness with Yourself

Honor The **G**ift In The Situation

You can use these ABCs to respond effectively to any situation. Here is information on how to do so:

Awaken Your Awareness of Stress: As you are noticing, through the work in this book, your thoughts are the cause of your stress. The exercises you have completed and are continuing to practice will help you understand when you begin causing yourself stress. Stress is not external, it is internal. There are always things we have to accomplish; there are always uncomfortable situations which arise. Stress is caused by our negative reactions to those things happening around us. When you awaken your awareness to understand that it is **you** who causes your own stress, you can better respond when faced with a difficult situation. This awareness is the first step. Without the awareness you cannot change your response. With this awareness you have an opportunity to take the next step in responding productively and preventing yourself from becoming overly stressed.

Breathe 3 Times and Focus: One of the quickest ways to decrease physical stress in the body is by breathing deeply. By taking three to ten deep breaths you can calm your nervous system to reduce your physical reaction. In fact, doctors I know at the Marino Center For Progressive Health in Wellesley, Massachusetts prescribe deep breathing to patients with high blood pressure. The doctors first measure a patient's blood pressure, then instruct the patient to breathe deeply for a few minutes. When they measure the patient's blood pressure after the deep breathing it is usually much lower. Thoughts and reactions form in our mind, causing our nervous system to launch into high gear and causing stress in the body. When we take 3 deep breaths we calm the physical reaction in our body. Using the practice of focusing in conjunction with breathing increases the positive results. Do this by letting your gaze rest on something that's in front of you or the person that's in front of you and notice everything you can about the object or the person. This reduces the grip of your thoughts and your stress reaction while enabling you to respond in the most effective way.

Call on Compassion: We have been training our minds to think since we were born. In our culture we are taught that we are most productive when we are thinking. However, most of this thinking does not make us more productive or effective. As we train ourselves to think less and be more present, we must be compassionate with ourselves because it is very hard to change this engrained habit. It **is** possible though, and that is why we are doing this work to learn how to change the negative engrained habits so we can be much more focused and effective in difficult situations. Have compassion for yourself by realizing this is hard and it goes against our cultural norms. When you find yourself thinking, "How did I get myself all caught up in this situation?

How did I fly off the handle?" say to yourself, "Well of course, this is a normal reaction in our culture, I spent my life so far reacting to everything that happened to me. I'm going to be patient with myself because I'm learning. I'm a student of this process and am learning, practicing and growing."

Don't Bite the Hook: Often when someone is upset or angry she is going to try to get you to bite the hook because she just wants to have a good argument. If you bite the hook, she feels good because she has gotten you to argue back with her and then she can state her point and win the argument. If you feel strongly about something, your emotions usually take over and you bite the hook. The next time you notice yourself starting to get pulled in, see whether you can stop it from happening. See whether you can say to yourself, "Nope I'm not going to get pulled into this. Even if I think that person is totally wrong and I want to argue my point, it is not worth it to me to bite the hook." An appropriate response may be, "I really don't want to discuss (argue) this with you right now."

One way to determine whether it is important to respond to an argument is to clarify your own top five values.

Try This: Identify Your Five Core Values

Take a moment to write your five core values. Consider: What do you feel strongly about? What is most important to you in life? What are your biggest priorities? Your list may include: trust, honesty, sincerity, joy, taking care of others, taking care of yourself, being authentic, being accurate or being available for loved ones. There are no right answers here. Write what feels most true in your heart.

Five Core Values

1. _____

2. _____

3. _____

4. _____

5. _____

Now that you know your five core values, think about a time when you chose to engage in a conversation because the topic or the issue was one of your five core values. Notice how you felt in that conversation. Maybe someone was questioning your trustworthiness and you feel very strongly about trust, so you engaged in that conversation. You bit the hook and marched full steam ahead to confront the issue. Most likely you felt strong and confident in this confrontation.

Now, remember a time when you bit the hook but it really wasn't one of your core values. Perhaps someone was trying to engage you in some sort of confrontation and you didn't want to be wrong so you argued your point. However, the topic wasn't one of your values. Notice how you felt in that argument. Most likely you felt like the confrontation wasn't going anywhere and was a waste of time, unless of course you like to argue just for argument's sake. Perhaps you regretted engaging in the argument.

The decision about whether to engage in confrontation is usually determined by whether you will authentically follow your values by participating. When you are trying to decide whether to engage, take a deep breath and try to respond without being emotionally charged. The way to do this is to state your point without caring whether you change the other person's opinion. In most cases we cannot change the other person's opinion anyway. You can then say to yourself, "I am going to let this go. I am not going to let this person affect me and pull me into this negative encounter."

Eliminate your story: Your initial reaction to any circumstance is just a reaction, all thoughts beyond the initial reaction become your story. Think about someone who did something you did not like. Your initial thought that you don't like what the person did is your negative reaction. When you begin thinking, "That person should never have done that to me. How dare him! He always does stuff like that. I hate him!" you have created a story about the person.

Eliminating the story reduces your stress. When you notice the negativity of the story, stop, focus on your breath and let the story dissipate. This can be difficult to do because we love stories and drama. The stories feel good to us and the drama is intriguing. We have become so comfortable in our own stories that we often don't recognize them. However, our own stories are often quite negative. Many of our negative thoughts originate from the stories ingrained in our minds because we repeat them so frequently.

Pema Chodron explains each story is like a groove on a record. Each time you think the story, the groove becomes deeper in your mind. However, you can reduce the grooves and even form new, more positive grooves. You do this by stopping each story as it comes up. Gradually you change the grooves in your brain and eventually you can stop the stories forever.

Find friendship and gentleness with yourself: Pema Chodron also teaches that it is impossible for us to find friendship and gentleness with others when we do not feel it for ourselves. Often the last person we are friendly or gentle with is ourselves. Think about what you say to yourself when you lose your car keys or forget something. Usually the first thought includes something about how stupid you are. Every time you say something negative or unkind to yourself, you send a message deep within that reinforces the negativity and stories already inside.

Try This: Lovingkindness Exercise

Let's see whether you can begin to find friendship and gentleness with yourself. One great way to do that is to begin a very simple and effective mental practice each morning called Lovingkindness. What follows is the first step of Lovingkindness practice which was taught to me by Sharon Salzberg, one of America's leading insight meditation teachers and spirituality writers. Repeat this 4 times silently:

- May I be safe

- May I be happy

- May I be healthy

- May I live with ease

Repeating these phrases each morning helps you to become aware of the thoughts you create for yourself and the way you may be too tough on yourself. You begin to be more kind to yourself. It also helps reduce your negative thoughts and stories so they are less likely to return during a difficult moment or difficult situation.

Honor the **G**ift in the situation: We will have difficult situations in our lives. No one lives a life unscathed. How we recover from difficult situations lies in our ability to find the gift or the blessing in the situation. Think back to the most difficult situation you ever experienced and see what gift was in that experience for you. One of my most challenging situations was taking care of my physically and mentally ill mother when she came to live with us. I had two young boys and felt completely and utterly overwhelmed (you can read more of this story in Appendix A). The gift for me in that situation was a realization that I had to do something for myself every day. This is how I began my daily meditation practice. This practice is now the first thing I do for myself each day. I have been dedicated to the practice since the beginning of 2005. There is rarely a day that I don't meditate.

My meditation practice is what keeps me healthy, relatively stress free and provides me with great insights each morning--it is the key to my life's work. If it hadn't been for that very difficult situation I probably would not have begun and sustained my meditation practice. Often times it takes something very challenging in life to inspire you to make real change. Sometimes you need something extremely difficult to happen to take you out of your daydream and help you see what change is needed.

Try This: Recognize The Gift

Take a moment to think of a very difficult time in your life. Describe the situation here:

_____

_____

_____

_____

_____

_____

What was the gift for you in this situation?

_____

_____

_____

_____

_____

_____

The 5 Biggest Stress Reduction Mistakes

As you work with the ABCs of Handling Difficult Situations, it is helpful to understand the five biggest mistakes people make in reducing their stress. This way you can make sure you are supporting yourself in reducing stress rather than sabotaging your efforts in some way. Here is the list:

1. Think It's 'One and Done'

2. Judge Their Progress

3. Beat Themselves Up

4. Don't Learn From Situations

5. Eat and Drink The Wrong Things

1. Think It's 'One and Done': Stress cannot be eliminated just by reading this book or by doing the practices for a week. To combat stress you must continually work on the techniques and allow them to support you each day. Take your 10 deep breaths every morning and every night before bed. If you can extend your morning breathing practice to 10 minutes, that is even better. Over time you will want to do your breathing practice each day and your day won't feel right if you have skipped it. You will begin to notice how much more effective you are because you are doing it--how much more effective you are in your personal relationships, your work, and how much less stress you feel. This is not a 'one and done', this is a life practice. It is you giving yourself a few minutes each day to increase your focus, productivity and effectiveness for each of the remaining minutes of your day.

2. Judge Their Progress--Let's say things go well for a while. You are able to stay pretty calm and make good decisions then, all of a sudden, you yell at your child or you blow up at someone at work. You then think, "Wow, I have spent three months breathing and I still blew up at someone. This obviously is not working." Try not to look at it this way. Your breathing **is** helping you, even if you didn't see it directly in this situation. You will get tested periodically--everyone does. It helps us see what we still need to work on and it encourages us to continue this breathing practice in order to make more progress.

Things will go smoothly for a while again, then you may notice you lose your cool again. You may wonder why you aren't making more progress. Looking at it this way is one of the biggest mistakes you can make. You have made progress just by doing the work. I am sure you will be able to look back to see all the ways in which your life has gotten better. When things don't go the way we think they should, these are great gifts for us. They teach us a lot more about ourselves than when everything goes smoothly.

3. Beat Themselves Up: Do not beat yourself up over things not going as well as you would like them to. If you do not act the way you want, take it as a learning opportunity and let the story end right there. Beating yourself up over something builds a negative story in your mind. We can see this with children--if I have a rough morning with my sons, they leave the house, go to school and don't think about it again. I, on the other hand, can stew over it all day long. They forgot it six hours ago and I beat myself up for six hours. The quickest way to stop beating yourself up is to say to yourself, "Okay what did I learn? Now I need to move on."

4. Don't Learn From Situations: When something doesn't go the way you want and you are able to stop beating yourself up, but you don't take the lesson from it, you are not able to apply what you learned in future situations. Sometimes the best and most powerful things we learn are lessons from the things that happen in our day to day life. I can give you lots of tools for reducing stress, however you are going to learn best from your own difficult situations. Take each lesson, learn from it and use it to your advantage.

5. Eat and Drink The Wrong Things: Processed foods, sugar and caffeine cause you to feel stressed. Just as your breath can calm your nervous system, food and drink can either calm or wire your nervous system. Caffeine, makes you feel wired and much more likely to snap, rush something you are working on and make a mistake. It is best to keep caffeine to a minimum so you can keep your body in a calmer state. When you consume processed food, sugar and caffeine, your system reacts and you negate many of the benefits of your breathing practice.

Processed foods have very low nutritional value. There are many additives in processed foods such as chemical preservatives, that our bodies were not designed to eat. It is only in the last 60 or 70 years that humans have ingested these chemicals. For thousands of years before that we were used to eating foods that were made of natural ingredients. Processed foods can cause mineral deficiencies and imbalances that make you retain water which in turn leads to weight gain. The food we eat immediately affects your body's energy. Natural foods boost your energy while processed foods deplete your energy.

Sugar jolts your nervous system, then sends you crashing down. Then you must eat more sugar or have caffeine to get back up to your baseline energy level. It becomes a vicious cycle. Sugar is also very disruptive to the nervous system and decreases your immunity. If you are concerned about catching a cold, stay away from sugar.

Reducing Stress Through Food

You can either reduce or increase stress through the food you eat. Just as thoughts come into our mind which affect our body and our energy, food affects both our nervous system and our energy.

David Zinczenko, the author of "Eat This, Not That!", wrote about categories of foods which are calming on the nervous system. I've added to each category some additional fruits and vegetables to give you more variety to choose from.

Vitamin C: In a University of Alabama study, 200 mg of vitamin C nearly stopped the stress hormones in rats. Researchers believe that if vitamin C can reduce the stress hormones in rats it can have the same impact on humans. We probably need much greater quantities. Some fruits and vegetables which are high in vitamin C are:

- red, orange and yellow bell peppers, brussels sprouts, kale, and broccoli

- oranges and kiwi

Peppermint: Peppermint can boost your performance and wake you up. Teachers are now giving peppermint to kids before they take state exams because kids have been shown to be more alert and to test better when they have had peppermint. One question I often get when I speak about peppermint is, "I assume peppermint patties do not count for the peppermint?" I don't suggest peppermint patties because they are so high in sugar which causes stress in the body. Out of the two, I'd recommend hard peppermint candy. The better forms of peppermint are:

- peppermint tea

- sniffing peppermint essential oil (which you can get at a health food store) will wake you up any time of the day

Magnesium: Magnesium decreases headaches, anxiety, tension, fatigue, blood pressure, nervousness and insomnia. In fact, there have been studies that show many people are deficient in magnesium. Some good sources are:

- Spinach, swiss chard and artichokes

- Black beans, soybeans, salmon, pumpkin seeds and almonds

Potassium: Potassium helps to reduce high blood pressure. Good sources of potassium are:

- Squash, spinach, papayas, bananas, and lentils

- Avocados have both potassium and healthy fatty acids that also help reduce high blood pressure

Omega-3 and Tryptophan: Omega-3 fat and tryptophan reduce levels of cortisol, the stress-inducing hormone in the body. Tryptophan is also sleep-promoting.

- Foods rich in omega-3: flax seeds, walnuts, sardines, halibut and salmon

- Foods rich in tryptophan: chicken, turkey, tuna, beef, soybeans and salmon

Vitamin E: Vitamin E decreases levels of stress hormones. Some good sources are:

- Sunflower seeds, olives, spinach, papaya and almonds.

Complex Carbohydrates: Healthy complex carbohydrates boost serotonin, which makes you feel cool, calm and in control. They also slow down digestion and prevent the energy low which accompanies the digestion of simple carbohydrates. Complex carbohydrates stay in your stomach longer, you feel satiated longer and your blood sugar stays level. Rather than having the energy high and the low, you will operate on a more even keel. When you are more even, your reaction to things won't be as emotional and as exaggerated. Good complex carbohydrates are:

- Quinoa, barley, whole wheat bread, oatmeal and brown rice.

Bottom line--eat natural foods and stay away from sugar and caffeine to help keep your nervous system calm and reduce stressful feelings and reactions.

Step 3 Homework

1. Breathe deeply 10 times each morning. You can increase your breathing practice to 5 minutes of breathing. Record your practice on the next page.

2. Breathe deeply 10 times right before bed.

3. Breathe deeply 3 times when stressed or when you notice yourself breathing shallowly.

4. Notice something in front of you when you are lost in thought.

5. Practice the ABC's in all challenging situations.

6. Don't judge your progress and don't beat yourself up.

7. Learn from every situation in your life.

8. Eat natural foods and reduce or eliminate processed foods, sugar and caffeine.

9. Do something that feeds your soul everyday.

10. Continue to notice thought patterns as they arise, what brought the pattern up, use your breath to dissolve the pattern and notice the outcome. Record your experience on the next page.

Homework - Step 3

Thought Pattern	Situation That Brought It Up	How You Dissolved Thought Pattern	Outcome

Place a ✓ for each day you practiced breathing:

Day 1	Day 2	Day 3	Day 4	Day 5	Day 6	Day 7

What did you notice this week?

Step 4: Make Important Life Changes

During the first three steps, we talked about the power of the mind, how we are often lost in thought and how we can bring ourselves back to the present moment using our breath. We also identified our limiting thought patterns and learned how to easily dissolve thought patterns and distractions through breath and through focus. We learned how to handle any situation productively and the biggest mistakes people make in trying to reduce stress.

I hope the daily practice of breathing and dissolving your limiting thoughts has made a difference in your life so far. Perhaps you feel more calm, focused, productive, more in control and less overwhelmed. Now is the perfect time to make lasting change in your life. You are primed to make great progress toward living life fully rather than merely letting life lead you.

Intention Statements

Think about how you intend to lead your life from this point forward. Now that you have more control over your thoughts and over your stress, how do wish to lead your life? What are your best qualities and how would you like to offer them to the world? What would you like to see flow to you, as a result?

Try This: Create a Life Intention Statement

Think about what two life intentions you would like to make. An intention statement is an expression of the deeper meaning for everything you do in life. With the awareness you gained doing the practices over the past few weeks, what deeper meaning do you want to incorporate into all future actions? What is your intention behind everything you will do from now on?

For example, your intention may be to be present and focused in every situation. You may intend to treat yourself and others with great respect. Or, you may intend to stop and breathe before reacting to any situation.

Take a moment to close your eyes and ask yourself about your deepest intentions. Write whatever comes to you. Don't worry about whether it sounds good or whether it's a valid intention. Just write whatever comes to mind.

It is my intention to:

_____

_____

_____

_____

It is my intention to:

_____

_____

_____

_____

Your intention statements are powerful. Place them in a few different spots so you'll see them every day, perhaps next to your bathroom mirror, on your computer or refrigerator, or in your car. A friend once had her goals taped right to her steering wheel. It was very powerful because she spent a lot of time in the car. She told me her intentions were realized that year. By seeing your intentions every day you will be sure to lead your life the way **you** want.

Try This: Create a Situational Intention Statement

Look at your homework pages from Steps 2 and 3. Choose two thought patterns that have arisen a number of times and look at the situations that brought them up. Notice how you dissolved the thought patterns and the outcome of your effort.

Write your intention for these specific situations. Your intention may be "to honor my relationship with_____" or "to truly listen to my mother" or "to recognize when my child is speaking to me and be fully available" or "to value the contribution _____ brings to the project." Focus on your two situations and write an intention for each.

It is my intention to:

_____

_____

_____

_____

It is my intention to:

_____

_____

_____

_____

You most likely have two very specific intentions now. They could have a big impact on your life if you follow your intentions and work on them. I suggest you also post these intentions next to your bathroom mirror, on your computer, or in your car. If they are related to someone who lives with you, you can exclude his or her name or post them in a place the other person won't see. You may even decide to tell the other person your intention if you think it will help your relationship.

For example, you could say to your child, "Jane, I know I don't always hear everything you say and it frustrates you. I'm going to try my best to hear what you say from now on. If you notice I'm distracted, would you please tell me?" This can be a terrific teaching point for a child. You'll earn their respect and show them we all need help being more available.

Improving Difficult Situations

Now, we are going to look at five situations in your life. Look back through your homework pages from Steps 2 and 3 or the Thought Pattern chart in Step 2 and choose five situations you would like to change in your life. They should be quite specific; the more specifically you name the situation the easier it'll be to do this exercise.

Try This: Improving Situations In Your Life

Choose five important situations in your life that you'd like to improve. Choose difficult situations that you would like to change in your life because you know they no longer serve you as they are. They can either be personal or professional situations. Perhaps it is a relationship with a child, your spouse, parents, co-worker, a manager, or with someone who reports to you. Perhaps one of your situations is your relationship with yourself--maybe you have a lot of negative thoughts about yourself.

Write these five situations in the left column of the chart on this page and next.

Situation	Ideal Situation
Confidence	
stay present	*fewer mistakes*

Situation	Ideal Situation

Next to each situation write how you'd like the situation to be instead. For example, if one of the situations is a strained relationship with a co-worker, the ideal situation is a mutually respectful working relationship in which you both contribute ideas and come up with creative and high quality projects. Use your senses to describe the ideal situation--write about how you'd like the situation to feel for you, what it would look like, what it might sound like and what you would see. Maybe it would even taste or smell differently. You know the expression, "I had a bad taste in my mouth"--would the ideal situation leave the same bad taste in your mouth? Putting as many details as you can in the ideal situation column will help you to better create that new situation in your life.

One other way to do this is to imagine it is a year from now and the situation is transformed. How does it feel to you, what conversations are now happening, what do you now see in the other person or what does the other person see in you?

This can be a challenging exercise because we tend to think that we do not have the power to change others, we can only control ourselves. This is very true. All we can control is ourselves. However, we often send negative feelings to others, effecting the situation, without realizing it. Brain research shows everyone has mirror neurons which instantly transmit our feelings to others and make us absorb other's feelings. It is instantaneous and completely out of our control. If we dislike working with a specific person, they feel this when they are with us and it negatively impacts the situation. When we change how we think about a situation, it often changes how someone behaves toward us and also how we perceive their actions.

When we change ourselves, we change the situation. Let me give an example of this. I know someone who had a relative with whom she didn't feel comfortable. She always felt the relative was sort of rude and did not like her. She felt excluded from group conversations in which this relative participated. She wanted to try to fix the situation and decided to begin recognizing all the great things about her relative. She recognized that her relative was very giving (perhaps not in the way she wanted, but giving nontheless) and quite funny in certain situations. This relative could also be counted on.

When this friend of mine started noticing these things about her relative, she noticed less the behaviors she didn't like. She then realized this relative is simply uncomfortable in certain situations. As a result, she was able to overlook what she interpreted as rudeness and instead took the initiative to speak with her and have a nice conversation. When she began acknowledging the many nice things the relative does and began to appreciate her for how she is, the relationship changed significantly.

When you change how you think about a person, you begin to see them differently. Then, they do act differently around you. Everything is your perception. Three people probably see three very different things in you. You can only control what you do and how you think of others. When you see the goodness in a person, and stop focusing on what you don't like, you can completely change your relationship with that person.

There is an excellent teacher, Byron Katie, who has created what she calls "The Work." She teaches an effective system for seeing situations differently. That friend of mine, I referred to on the last page, had a session with Byron Katie and "The Work" is what completely changed her relationship with her relative. You can learn more about Byron Katie's work and have a free session with someone trained by Byron Katie herself by visiting her website: *thework.com*. I would recommend, if you have a challenging person in your life, you do "The Work" about your relationship with this person and see what happens. It's extremely powerful and effective.

Returning to your ideal situation, imagine your most difficult situation turned into an ideal situation. Look back at what you wrote about your ideal situations and imagine that you love to see those people and enjoy the situations. What would those situations look like? See whether you can stop thinking about what you want to change about the people and, instead, imagine how it would be if you truly enjoyed being with them exactly as they are.

Afformation Statements

Noah St. John coined the term "afformation statements" in his book, *The Secret Code of Success*. You have probably heard of affirmation statements in which you say something that you hope will happen. For example, "My relationship with my relative is loving and joyful." Then your brain says, "Yeah right! That's not possible." St. John explains the problem with affirmation statements is that if we try to convince our brain that something is so, our brain rationalizes why it isn't so and keeps us locked right where we are. We never realize lasting change this way.

Our brain is always trying to figure out what is true and how to make things work. Our brains do really well with this type of thinking. If you have a problem or situation you are working through, your brain can tackle the problem and figure out all the steps needed to make it happen. St. John says afformation statements let us use our brain the way it works best. Afformation statements are statements about something you'd like to be true in your life. When they are stated a certain way, the mind figures out how to create the positive change in your life to make the statement true.

Try This: Writing Afformation Statements

Go back to the ideal situations in the **Improving Situations In Your Life** exercise and give each ideal situation a short title, like "I enjoy my coworker." Write these short titles on the left side of this chart on this page and the next page.

For each of these ideal situations, write an afformation statement. An afformation statement is a question about why the situation is true. For example, "Why is my relationship with this co-worker so easy?" or "Why is this project so successful?" Start with the situations that are easiest to imagine and then move on to the more difficult situations and write your afformation.

Ideal Situation	Afformation Statement

Ideal Situation	Afformation Statement

When you write afformations, your brain automatically comes up with ways to make it happen, to make it true. You'll get great ideas for making progress in these situations.

Let's take this one step further. Now that you have your afformation statements, let's get your brian to fill in the blanks and tell you what you need to do to make them true.

Try This: Next Steps

Transfer the afformation statements you created above into the left column of this chart. Ask yourself, "For this to be true, what needs to happen?" Write these answers next to each afformation statement in the Next Steps column.

For example, let's use the afformation statement, "Why is my relationship with this co-worker so easy?" Your Next Steps could be:

• I appreciate his attention to detail

• I ask him how his weekend was

• I realize he has a challenging job and that he's just trying to do it the best he can

- I help him out from time to time by giving him some information which will help make his job easier

Afformation Statement	Next Steps

Now you have a list of some great next steps to take in making some situations in your life more pleasant and even enjoyable.

Bringing It All Together

Now I'm going to ask you to review the exercises you completed in this chapter and write a little about how they make you feel. This is very important because it helps you tap into a new way of feeling about your life and the difficult situations you are experiencing. When you tap into these new feelings, you are able to move ahead toward making them reality.

Go back and read your Life Intention Statements. How do you feel after stating your intentions? Write a few sentences about how reading your statements makes you feel:

_____

_____

_____

_____

_____

_____

_____

_____

Read your Situational Intention Statements. How do you feel after stating these intentions? Write a few sentences about how reading your statements makes you feel:

_____

_____

_____

_____

_____

_____

_____

Are there some specific ways you can fulfill both your life and situational intentions each day? What can you do starting tomorrow to fulfill those intentions?

Beginning tomorrow I can do the following to fulfill my Life Intentions:

_____

_____

_____

_____

_____

Beginning tomorrow I can do the following to fulfill my Situational Intentions:

_____

_____

_____

_____

_____

_____

Read your Ideal Situations and your Afformation Statements. How do you feel? Write a few sentences about how reading your Ideal Situations and Afformation Statements makes you feel:

_____

_____

_____

_____

_____

_____

Read your Afformation Statements and Next Steps. How do you feel? Write a few sentences about how reading your Afformation Statements and Next Steps makes you feel:

_____

_____

_____

_____

_____

_____

Did any new next steps come to mind? Jot down any new ideas you have after re-reading your afformation statements:

_____

_____

_____

_____

_____

_____

_____

_____

Step 4 Homework

Much of the homework this week is the same as the past weeks because you are still working on forming these practices into good habits.

1. Breathe deeply 10 times each morning. You can increase your breathing practice to 10 minutes of breathing. Record your practice on the next page.

2. Breathe deeply 10 times right before bed.

3. Breathe deeply 3 times when stressed or when you notice yourself breathing shallowly.

4. Notice something in front of you when you are lost in thought.

5. Practice the ABC's in all challenging situations.

6. Don't judge your progress and don't beat yourself up.

7. Learn from every situation in your life.

8. Eat natural foods and reduce or eliminate processed foods, sugar and caffeine.

9. Do something that feeds your soul everyday.

10. Continue to notice thought patterns as they arise, what brought the pattern up, use your breath to dissolve the pattern and notice the outcome. Record your experience on the next page.

11. Post your Life Intention Statements, Situational Intention Statements, Afformation Statements and Next Steps in a place where you'll see them twice each day. Read through them, while breathing deeply, in the morning and the evening.

Homework - Step 4

Thought Pattern	Situation That Brought It Up	How You Dissolved Thought Pattern	Outcome

Place a ✓ for each day you practiced breathing:

Day 1	Day 2	Day 3	Day 4	Day 5	Day 6	Day 7

What did you notice this week?

Step 5: Employ The 7 Habits Of Conscious Success

In the first step we talked about the power of the mind and how often we become lost in thought. We learned how to use our breath to bring our attention back to the present moment.

In the second step, we identified limiting thought patterns that play over and over in our mind. We practiced noticing when they come up during the day and dissolving them.

In the third step, we learned how to handle difficult situations effectively and in the fourth step, we set the stage for intentional living. We can now move forward to living life rather than being lived by life.

The fifth and final step is incorporating the Seven Habits of Conscious Success.

But first I'd like to share the results of a study which explain why it is so important to reduce the wandering of your mind. The *New York Times* wrote about a study on November 15, 2010 which was also published in *Science*, in which a Harvard psychologist named Dr. Gilbert contacted people around the world at random intervals to ask what they were doing, what they were thinking about and how they were feeling.

They found most peoples' minds were wandering at least 30% of the time, and as much as 65% of the time. On average, throughout the quarter of a million responses, peoples' minds were wandering 47% of the time. Dr. Gilbert said, "I find it kind of weird now to look down the crowded street and realize that half the people aren't really there."

They found no correlation between the joy of the activity and the pleasantness of someone's thoughts. For example, if someone was doing something they deemed enjoyable, their thoughts weren't necessarily happy.

Dr. Gilbert says, "Even if you are doing something that is really enjoyable, that doesn't seem to protect against negative thoughts. The rate of mind wandering is lower for more enjoyable activities but when people wander, they are just as likely to wander toward negative thoughts."

The researchers found that whatever people were doing, they tended to be happier if they were focused on the activity instead of thinking about something else. Whether their minds were wandering was a better predictor of happiness than what they were doing.

Dr. Gilbert said, "The study suggests that the location of the body is much less important than the location of the mind, and the location of the body has surprisingly little influence on the location of the mind. The heart goes where the head takes it and neither cares much about the whereabouts of the feet."

Here is clear evidence that the wandering mind causes unhappiness. The researchers went on to say, "The unhappiness produced by mind wandering was largely the result of thought episodes involving unpleasant topics. Such stray thoughts make people more miserable than commuting or working or any other activity." They found people having stray thoughts on neutral topics ranked only a little below the overall average in happiness. Those who were dreaming about pleasant topics were actually a bit above the average, although not as happy as people who's minds were not wandering.

Even if you are daydreaming about something good, you're still not going to be as happy as if your mind is not wandering at all. The researchers found, over several months of the study, the more frequent mind wanderers remained less happy than the rest of the group. The researchers said the moral of the study is, "You stray, you pay."

This study reinforces how important it is to keep your mind focused on the present moment--not only for productivity and to be effective in your interactions--but in order to be happy and enjoy your life.

We have identified Seven Actions that create success in your personal and professional life when combined with the other practices in this book. These Seven Actions offer you ways to act which enhance your clarity and purpose. They are:

The Seven Actions of Conscious Success

1. Be Present

2. Pay It Forward

3. Understand Others

4. Clearly Communicate

5. Embrace Differences

6. Share Your Expertise

7. Learn From Others

1. **Be Present**: Being present is the single most effective thing you can do to be on top of your game. By being focused on the task or conversation at hand you will be much more creative and effective and you will come up with better solutions. You will be able to discern the deeper meaning of a situation to create the best outcome. To be present, use the strategies you have been practicing to bring yourself back to the current moment whenever you notice your mind wandering.

2. **Pay It Forward**: Do something that will help someone else. For example, when asked to do a project, do that project plus a little more. Try to

make the next person's job a little easier by giving them additional information. In addition to providing the data, give your thoughts on what you think the data means.

3. **Understand Others**: We want to be understood and so does everyone else. Too often, we are so determined to get our point across that we don't hear what the other person is really saying. Rather, if you approach your interactions with an intent to listen to and understand others, you better understand the situation and you are able to respond more appropriately. Listen first, ask questions and offer a solution only after you fully understand the situation. Make an attempt to fully understand your clients, vendors, colleagues, manager, friends and family members. Try to really understand those who support you and those who work for you. You will gain real insight and will know how best to act in any situation.

4. **Clearly Communicate**: As you listen to others, make sure your communication is clear and easily understood by others. You can do this by checking with the other person. Ask, "Am I being clear?" Ask the person to tell you what they heard you say. Keep the conversation going until you are sure the person clearly understands what you are trying to communicate.

5. **Embrace Differences**: In every organization, there are a wide variety of personalities, skills and abilities. This variety makes the organization successful. In addition, the variety of personalities, skills and abilities around you make you successful. The more you embrace everyone's differences, the more easily you will work with others and the more successful you will be. If there is someone who rubs you the wrong way, focus on their good qualities. Perhaps they are very detailed, perhaps they keep everyone on task or perhaps they are very creative. Focusing

on the way the person bothers you is simply a waste of time and reduces your effectiveness.

6. **Share Your Expertise**: The more you share your expertise with others, the more you'll be seen as a valued person and the more you can help your organization. When you share your expertise in a helpful way for others, your colleagues will want to work with you more often and see the value you bring. Don't keep your expertise bottled up inside. Don't view it as something that can be taken away from you. Instead, sharing your expertise can be a way of furthering your advancement by helping others or making your team better.

7. **Learn From Others**: When you approach a working relationship or a meeting with the desire to learn, you are automatically more open to understanding others and they are more open to understanding you. When someone feels you want to hear them and learn from them, they will share the most helpful information they have and in turn they will be open to learning from you.

Think about how you can use these seven actions throughout your day. Use the space below to write some concrete ways you can use each habit:

1. Be Present: In which situations or with which people can you be more present?

_____

_____

_____

_____

_____

_____

2. Pay It Forward: How can you help some people out or offer more value in your work and projects?

_____

_____

_____

_____

_____

3. Understand Others: Who can you better understand? How can you listen better?

_____

_____

_____

_____

_____

4. Clearly Communicate: How can you be clearer in your communication? With whom can you be clearer?

_____

_____

_____

_____

_____

5. Embrace Differences: How can you put aside your differences and see the positive in others? What positive qualities does a co-worker or family member have?

_____

_____

_____

_____

_____

_____

6. Share Your Expertise: What specific point of view or expertise do you have that is helpful for others? In what situations can you share your knowledge?

_____

_____

_____

_____

_____

_____

7. Learn From Others: Who can you learn from? How can you learn from more people in general?

_____

_____

_____

_____

_____

_____

Try the 7 Actions in many different situations and with different people, both personally and professionally. Notice how they transform your interactions with other people and help you to be perceived more positively.

Step 5 Homework

Continue using these techniques and making them a normal part of your day. Use them so they become habit and second nature when you encounter a stressful situation.

1. Breathe deeply 10 times each morning. You can increase your breathing practice to 10 minutes of breathing. Record your practice on the next page.

2. Breathe deeply 10 times right before bed.

3. Breathe deeply 3 times when stressed or when you notice yourself breathing shallowly.

4. Notice something in front of you when you are lost in thought.

5. Practice the ABC's in all challenging situations.

6. Don't judge your progress and don't beat yourself up.

7. Learn from every situation in your life.

8. Eat natural foods and reduce or eliminate processed foods, sugar and caffeine.

9. Do something that feeds your soul everyday.

10. Continue to notice thought patterns as they arise, what brought the pattern up, use your breath to dissolve the pattern and notice the outcome. Record your experience on the next page.

11. Read your Life Intention Statements, Situational Intention Statements, Afformation Statements and Next Steps while breathing deeply in the morning and the evening.

12. Begin practicing the Seven Actions of Conscious Success by acting on the notes you took in this chapter.

Homework - Step 5

Thought Pattern	Situation That Brought It Up	How You Dissolved Thought Pattern	Outcome

Place a ✓ for each day you practiced breathing:

Day 1	Day 2	Day 3	Day 4	Day 5	Day 6	Day 7

What did you notice this week?

Cementing Positive Change

We have covered a large amount of information and hopefully you've practiced the techniques enough so they are becoming second nature. The key to creating lasting positive change is to continue the practice of the techniques until they become your natural solution to any stressful or difficult situation. When you practice them each day, over time they will automatically be your default solution.

The Key To Success
Practice, Practice, Practice

1. Breathe Deeply 10 Times Each Morning (Even Better Try 5-10 Minutes Of Meditation - see Appendix A) Use the Logs in Appendix B to keep you on track

2. Breathe Deeply 10 Times Right Before Bed

3. Breathe Deeply 3 Times When Stressed Or When Breathing Shallowly

4. Notice Something In Front Of You When Lost In Thought

5. Practice The ABCs In All Challenging Situations

6. Eat Stress Fighting Foods and Eliminate Stress Causing Foods and Drinks

7. Do Something That Feeds Your Soul Every Day

Let's face it, we're all busy. You may not be able to practice each of these techniques daily or you may forget to use them when in a challenging situation. However, if you begin each day with your morning breathing practice, you will set yourself up for the greatest success. Think of your daily breathing practice as putting on a parachute. Just as you wouldn't jump out of a plane without a parachute, don't begin your day without re-calibrating your nervous system. This breathing practice gives you a solid foundation; when you are caught off guard or put into a difficult situation, you can recover more quickly and are much more likely to remember to use your breath to gain control of the situation. By calming your nervous system each morning, you are less likely to fly off the handle during the day.

If you can extend your breathing to five to ten minutes in the morning, your life will change. Your stress will reduce significantly. Your outlook on life will be more positive. You will have trained your brain to refocus quickly, thus enhancing your life and helping you to decrease stress throughout your day. See Appendix A for tips on how to extend your practice in this way.

Taking ten deep breaths as you lie down in bed at night helps you to go to sleep more easily and sleep more soundly during the night. It may even prevent you from waking up in the middle of the night.

Breathing deeply three times when you are stressed or when you notice you are breathing shallowly resets your nervous system and reduces stress levels during the day. Take a little inventory right now, are you breathing shallowly? Is your breath only filling the top third of your lungs? If so, take a deep belly breath. Notice how good it feels.

Take a moment to think about what moments during your day you tend to breathe most shallowly. Is it during commuting? Is it during a particular meeting? Is it talking to a particular person? Make an effort to take at least three deep breaths during these situations over the next few days to train yourself to automatically deepen your breath when it becomes shallow.

When do you tend to become most lost in thought during your day? Make an effort to notice something in front of you when that happens. Perhaps it is when talking to your child or a co-worker? Focus on that person's eyes when you notice your mind wandering. This will greatly enhance your connection to the person and make the conversation more rewording and productive.

Practice the ABCs in challenging situations. Go back to the Negative Thought Pattern Exercise in Step 2 and see whether you are less challenged by the situations in your 'Likely Situations' column. Use STOP and the ABCs from Step 3 when you find yourself challenged by situations.

Try to make a real effort to eat stress fighting foods and eliminate stress causing foods and drinks. Take a look at the list in Step 3 and notice whether you are incorporating more of these stress fighting foods and see whether you've been able to eliminate some caffeine, sugar and processed food from your diet. Determine which foods you still want to add to your diet. See whether you can cut further back on stress causing foods and drinks. With each small change you will feel better and have more energy throughout your day.

Do something that feeds your soul every day. Refer to the Feed Your Soul exercise in Step 1. This is a list you created of the things that feed your soul. Make sure you do at least one of them every day. This is very important. Periodically, I'll have a day where I can't fit in something from my 'Feed My Soul List.' By the end of those days I feel frustrated, tired and overall in a funk. On one such frustrating day, I backed out of a minor commitment at the end of the day and did a half hour of yoga. After the yoga, I felt so much better. I was able to make dinner for my family and have a great evening. Taking a half hour to do yoga fed me. Where before I felt empty of anything to give and irritable, after feeding myself with yoga, I was able to then feed everyone else by making dinner and having a fun evening. This process of feeding ourselves is very powerful.

Commitment To Your Growth

Try This - Commitment To Your Growth

Now it is time to make a true commitment to yourself--a commitment to your growth as a person. Write down the practices you want to make sure you will use going forward. Indicate the techniques you intend to use to help you reduce stress and be more present. For example, let's say you are going to do some deep breathing each morning and each evening, write that you will do daily, at what time of day and for how many minutes.

I commit to using the following practices going forward (include frequency and timing):

1. _____

   _____

2. _____

   _____

3. _____

   _____

4. _____

   _____

5. _____

   _____

6. _____

   _____

7. _____

_____

The most important thing for me to remember in managing my stress is:

_____

_____

_____

_____

So far, I've made progress in this area:

_____

_____

_____

_____

I look forward to making more progress in these areas:

_____

_____

_____

_____

Signature:_____

Date:_____

By signing this, you are making a commitment to yourself. Copy this and post both pages some place where you will see them each day. Take this commitment to yourself seriously, just as seriously as commitments you make to anyone else.

Remember, you control your stress and your nervous system through your focus and your breath. Just as you can increase your stress and reduce focus by breathing shallowly and being lost in thought, you can decrease stress and increase focus by breathing deeply.

If you want more results learn how to begin and sustain a 10-minute meditation practice. See Appendix A for instructions.

Use the Breathing and Meditation Practice Logs in Appendix B to keep you on track and help you ensure your practice becomes a habit.

You are in charge. No one else can cause you stress. You may experience challenging situations, but it is your reaction which causes stress for yourself.

Whenever you notice things aren't going the way you would like them too, you can always change your experience by taking a deep breath and focusing on your breath.

You have the power to control your life and to make your experience positive. You have control over your nervous system with your breath and with the foods and drinks you consume. Remember, you can find happiness and peace in any moment by focusing on your breath.

You are in control and **you** have the
power to make your life great!

I wish you much success and encourage you to take
full control of your life.
May you soar to new great heights!

Please share your success with me at:
Jacqueline@ConsciousSuccess.net

Resources

This book is a compilation of the mindfulness teachings I've learned and integrated in my life. Many great teachers have contributed to my learning. Here are some of their names--I'd recommend any books they've written.

- Pema Chodron, her audio CDs, books and videos are terrific!

- Eckhart Tolle, he did a great series of on-line classes about the content of his book, *A New Earth,* with Oprah Winfrey. You might be able to find them on Oprah's website. It was really powerful to hear and see them talk about being present.

- Jon Kabat-Zinn

- Byron Katie--her website thework.com is especially helpful if you have disagreements with certain people in your life or you find certain people very difficult.

- Eknath Easwaran

- Lama Surya Das

- Thich Nhat Hanh

- Adyshanti

- Daniel Goleman, author of *Emotional Intelligence* and *Working With Emotional Intelligence,* among numerous other books.

- Sharon Salzberg

- Erich Schiffmann

- Sarah Powers

"Meditation has been integral in my career; it is the single best thing that happened to me in terms of my leadership. Meditation enables one to focus on what is really important; and I haven't had high blood pressure since the 1970s."

~Bill George, Professor of Management Practice at Harvard Business School

"If you have a meditation practice, you can be much more effective in a meeting, meditation helps develop your abilities to focus better and to accomplish your tasks."

~Robert Stiller, Chairman, Green Mountain Coffee

"Meditation helps to create calm at will or focus at will, that's something you need to be able to do if there are millions of dollars at stake."

~Maria Gonzalez, President of Toronto-based Argonauta Strategic Alliances Consulting Inc.

Appendix A: Realizing Even Greater Results By Meditating

If you are enjoying the techniques in this book and would like to realize even greater results, learning to meditate is the perfect next step.

Meditation provides something akin to a parachute--a backup safety system when navigating your daily experience. With a daily meditation practice under your belt you will more likely remember to use your breath when encountering a difficult situation. Your daily practice offers you a safety net and more resiliency.

Resiliency is important. We have little control over what happens to us--the car crash, the sickness, the death of a loved one--however, the amount of resiliency we have determines how we handle these difficult situations.

The Principal of our Middle School recommended we read, "The Optimistic Child" written by Martin E. P. Seligman, Ph.D.. Dr. Seligman explains a person's level of pessimism directly correlates to how likely they are to suffer from depression. The studies he has done show that a person who is optimistic has a resiliency that reduces the likelihood of suffering from depression.

In my opinion, from my experience, meditation is a great tool for building optimism and resiliency. It offers clarity and a new perspective from which I can lead my life each day.

Why Meditate?

As we age, the right frontal lobe (pre-frontal cortex) of our brain becomes smaller and less active. The right pre-frontal cortex is the part of the brain in which we feel compassion and create ideas. As this area shrinks, we find we are more cranky, more critical and have fewer creative ideas. You may have noticed that as people get older they are crankier and more set in their ways. This is due, in part, to this area of the brain shrinking and becoming less active.

Meditation has shown, in a study at the University of Wisconsin in conjunction with Harvard University, that a regular meditation practice can increase the activity in the pre-frontal cortex and even increase the size of this part of the brain. When you feed the right frontal lobe with meditation, you will feel more compassionate and less cranky. You will also notice that your stress levels are reduced because meditation also calms the nervous system.

Meditation also boosts your immune system. Sometimes this reason is the one that gets me out of bed to meditate when I am feeling run down or sick.

Some of the other benefits people experience with a daily meditation practice are:

- calm awareness
- reduced blood pressure
- peaceful feelings
- increased concentration and focus
- greater ability to be present
- life feels less hectic
- more inspiration and connection to intuition
- a clearer mind--less groggy with more energy

Meditation is exercise for the mind. It offers a great way to practice bringing attention back to the present moment. Beginning each day with a daily meditation practice creates a buffer for the day. Things tend to bother us less.

If you're like me, you wake up with an immediate 'To Do List' in your head. Mine has at least 20 items on it everyday. Many of the items can't even be completed in one day--how overwhelming! After meditation, my 'To Do List' shrinks to the 3-5 most important items--all of which I can usually easily handle that day. My large, overwhelming projects are replaced with some specific items that will move the project forward and are vital to making progress on the project.

My Meditation Story

In 2004 I practiced yoga each morning in our living room. It was great for me since at the time I had two energetic young boys. After my practice, I felt calm, energized and ready for the day.

Then, in early 2005, I traveled three quarters of the way across the country to get my mom who needed to come live with us because her physical health was waning and her dementia had progressed to the point where she couldn't take care of herself. She had lost a lot of weight and weighed only 85 pounds.

Back at our house, my mom slept in a bedroom on our first floor very close to our living room. My morning yoga practice was now impossible because my mom needed my help as soon as I came downstairs. However, I knew I needed to do something each morning to manage the pressure I was under. I decided to try meditating. I told my husband and boys that I would sit still for 10 minutes each day. They could come and go from the room and my boys were welcome sit on my lap, but I was going to be silent during that time.

At first, it was quite difficult. It's hard to sit still for 10 minutes when there are so many things to do! I had a lot to do in a short time. I had to sell my mom's house from a great distance, decide what to do with all her belongings, sell her car, look after her care in our house and manage her multiple hospitalizations. All of this, on top of the responsibilities of running a household, taking care of two young boys and trying to have some energy left over to enjoy time with my husband. How could I take time every day to just sit?

Deep down I knew that if I didn't meditate for 10 minutes each day, I would lose my mind. So, I sat each morning. I had made the commitment to myself and I did not skip a day. Those 10 minutes were just about the only time I had for myself each day.

Some days meditation felt great, other days, it felt like a huge waste of time. I kept it going though because I had read that even if my mind was wandering like crazy, the act of sitting and trying to meditate was the important part. Meditating each day would be a great benefit for me, even if it didn't feel like I was making any progress.

Some days my body was itching to get up, my legs would fall asleep or I'd feel a pain in a part of my body. Meditation teachers said to breathe with whatever I was feeling and, sure enough, the sensations went away. Sometimes I did need to stretch out a leg, but I continued meditating even with one leg sticking out of the blanket because I had made a commitment to myself that I knew I needed to honor.

A few months into my practice, during a particularly stressful time--my Mom almost died twice in the hospital and each day I dragged my boys through the long sterile corridors to see her because we never knew which day would be her last--I knew the benefits were being felt by my family. My four-year-old son said to me, "Mommy, did you meditate today? Because you're being really good."

That's all I needed to hear to continue my practice. I was feeling a little better and was getting through this extremely difficult time without completely losing it, so I knew the meditation practice was helping me. I was pleased that my son had noticed the benefits as well.

I continue to meditate to this day. I've tried different practices at various points throughout the years and often come back to a practice called Shamatha, which means "mindfulness."

I have allowed the time I spend in meditation to grow naturally. I began with ten minutes every morning and often had to look over at the clock a few times until I reached the ten minute mark. Now, I sit down and at the end of my practice find I have been sitting anywhere from 30-50 minutes.

What I've learned is that if you set an intention for how long you want to sit, you usually end up sitting that long. Some days I only have 20 minutes and by setting that intention, I'm able to limit it to that amount of time.

Now, let's try a five minute meditation (go to the next page)...

Try This: Five Minute Meditation

Sit with your back straight. Your eyes can be opened or closed. If your eyes are open, let your eyes rest gently on something a few feet in front of you. If they are closed, let them gently look up to the inside of your forehead. If your eyes are active, your mind will be active.

You might notice it is a challenge to stop the movement of your eyes. If so, this tells you that your mind is quite active. If it is hard to focus your eyes, know that over time it will get easier. You can practice slowing your eyes down when doing your daily activities. As you are talking to someone in person or on the phone let your eyes gently focus on something in front of you or on the person. This will quiet your mind, bring focus to your conversation and help you practice quieting your mind throughout your day.

If your eyes are open, during the meditation let them blink as you do in conversation. Let your hands rest on your thighs or your knees. Now simply breathe and feel your breath in your body or at the tip of your nose.

Let your breath flow in and out easily. Notice your exhalations. Let your exhalations be an example of letting go. Just as you let go of your breath, allow your mind to let go of thoughts.

When you find yourself thinking, say "thinking" silently to yourself in a kind, compassionate tone and go back to noticing your breathing.

Breath this way for 5 minutes.

After five minutes, take a few deep breaths and, if your eyes are closed, slowly open them to notice the room around you.

Meditation opens you up to connecting more deeply to your intuition. Does your mind feel more calm? Did you gain any insight during your meditation? If so, write it down here:

_____

_____

_____

How To Begin And Sustain Your Meditation Practice

To make meditation a habit, be consistent:

The Same:

Place

Time

Technique

Commit to sit each day for 10 minutes.

Sit in a comfortable position with your back straight.

Sit in the same place each day.

Set up a corner with pillows, use a comfortable chair, sit on your bed or find any place that is comfortable.

Begin your practice at about the same time each day.

Tell yourself you will sit and breathe for 10 minutes.

When your mind wanders say, "Thinking" silently to yourself and bring your mind back to your breath.

Don't judge any of your meditation sessions.

If you do have to miss a day, begin again the very next day.

Practice each day and you'll soon notice the life-changing results!

Practice your meditation at the **same time** each day. It may be upon awakening in the morning, before you go to bed at night, after the kids leave the house, right when you get home from work, or right before dinner. Decide what time will work best for you and make a commitment to yourself to sit for 10 minutes at roughly that same time every day.

Sit in the **same place** for your practice every time. Create a place in your home where you do your meditation practice. You may sit on the edge of your bed, on pillows with your legs crossed, in your favorite chair, or on pillows in the corner. Wherever it is, go to that same place each time you meditate. By keeping your meditation practice at the same time and the same place each day, it easily becomes a habit. Over time your body and mind simply gravitate toward sitting in that place, at that time each day.

After a few weeks or a month, you'll find yourself thinking, "When I get home tonight I'm taking ten minutes for myself to meditate" or "When I get up in the morning, I'm going to meditate for ten minutes on my bed." It will become habit and you will **want** to do it. After a while, you will find you rely on your practice to rejuvenate you and that your practice feels really good.

It is also important to use the **same technique,** at least for awhile. The technique you just tried is a traditional Buddhist meditation technique, called Shamatha or mindfulness. It is a practice of focusing on your breath, exactly the same way you have been noticing your breath in Steps 1-5.

At different times, you may be inspired to try a different meditation technique--this is perfectly normal and fine. I've used different techniques at some points during my years of practice and they've been particularly helpful and inspiring at those times. Some different techniques are: reciting a prayer or mantra, incorporating different types of breath work (called pranayama), or using different hand positions or mudras. However, when you begin your practice, it is important to commit to one technique until your practice is firmly in place. This usually takes six months to a year.

Shamatha is a terrific meditation practice. It helps you to gain awareness of the thoughts that run through your mind. Throughout it you practice returning your focus to the present moment. It is training for your mind and gives you the ability to be much more present in your daily life.

Committing To Your Own Meditation Practice

Congratulations on taking this first step toward increasing your wellness and health! To begin your meditation practice take a moment to write down your commitment to yourself.

Here's what your commitment might look like, "I commit to meditating for 10 minutes each day for at least one month." My commitment:

_____

_____

Here's what your 'why' might look like, "I am committing to this daily meditation practice to help myself become clearer, less stressed and to reduce my blood pressure." My why:

_____

_____

_____

_____

Where do you plan to sit each day? My Where:

_____

_____

When do you plan to sit each day? My When:

_____

_____

What practice to you intend to use? You can use Shamatha or, if you've been taught a different technique, you can use that practice. My What:

_____

Additional Meditation Tips

- At the beginning of each practice remind yourself of your commitment for that practice. For example, "I will sit for ten minutes and breathe right now."

- Feel your breath as it fills your body. Feel it go in and out of your body, do not worry about the quality of the breath, just notice your breath.

- Whenever you notice your mind wandering say, "Thinking" silently, gently and compassionately to yourself, and bring your mind back to your breath. Your brain is meant to think so do not get upset with yourself if you find yourself thinking a lot. Remember, you are re-training your mind. Simply bring your mind back to your breath whenever it wanders. Every time you notice it wandering, gently guide your mind back to your breath.

- Don't judge any of your meditation sessions. A session in which you are able to stay pretty quiet most of the time is no better than a session in which your mind keeps wandering off and you have to bring it back. In fact, the session in which you have to keep bringing your mind back to your breath can be even more productive because you get good practice coming back to the present moment.

- An easy way to bring your mind back to your breath is by trying to feel your breath in your body. Allow your breath to become deep as you feel it, without forcing it.

- Periodically you can look to the clock to see how long you've been sitting. After a while, you will automatically look at the clock after the full 10 minutes.

- At the end of your 10 minute session, notice how you feel. You might feel more calm, clearer, or have less anxiety, worry, or fear.

- If you have a session in which you sit down, your mind wanders off and you don't even notice it has wandered until you are nine minutes into your meditation, don't beat yourself up. Just know that's what had to happen that day. At least you are able to bring yourself back after nine minutes. That's quite a feat because when you get nine minutes into a thought, you are pretty deeply rooted in the scenario you have created in your mind. Being able to notice the thought at that point is terrific.

- Buddhist meditation teachers refer to the mind as a wild monkey. We've let our minds run free our entire life. If you imagine the room you are in right now with a monkey swinging from corner to corner and all over the place--what a mess your room would be after only a minute of that monkey being in there! Now, think how your life could look differently without your wild "monkey mind" running the show. When we begin to gain control of this "monkey mind" we begin to experience more serenity, less stress, more inspiration, more calm, and less anger, sadness, fear and anxiety.

- If you have to miss a day, begin again the very next day. Don't skip more than one day.

Meditation Q&A

Here are some of the best questions I've received regarding meditation.

- *"Isn't it good to think? Are you suggesting that we shouldn't think or try to figure out solutions to our problems?"*

    There certainly are times in which thinking about your problems is important. However, when you are not working on the problem, don't let your problem take over your life by thinking about it all of the time. Set specific time aside for problem solving. Make sure you spend this time just brainstorming about that situation. When you are working on a problem be in the present moment fully with it.

    Likewise, when you are talking to someone, let your whole attention be on talking to that person. When you are out taking a walk, let your whole attention be on the things around you on that walk. When you're driving in a car, let your whole attention be on driving so that you are safe.

    When you begin segmenting your focus in this way you have better communication with others. You will also notice that when your mind is less busy with thinking, you have more clarity and more creative solutions pop into your head for all areas of your life.

    We usually come up with the best solutions when we are not so busy thinking about the problem. Have you ever noticed you get your best ideas when you are in the shower or exercising? When your mind is clear, your best solutions emerge.

- *"Meditation is really hard for me. I don't know whether I can do this. What do you suggest?"*

    Meditation can be hard. If this is the case, first commit to practicing for seven days-- without expectation that you are even going to do it beyond the seven days. Just sit and notice your breath for ten minutes everyday. If it's very hard for you, just sit as long as you can. If your mind is wandering all the time, that's okay--bring it back when you notice it. Just sit. We're not striving for a crystal clear mind, we are simply striving for sitting and breathing for 10 minutes each day.

    Sometimes getting your hands involved can be very helpful. With each breath touch your thumb to the tip of a different finger. Doing something kinesthetic can help calm your mind and make it easier to sit.

- *"Will meditation really get good results for me. What will it do for me?"*

    Meditation has some very tangible benefits. The primary one is clarity. Upon waking the brain usually immediately kicks in and begins thinking about everything that needs to happen that day. This creates real stress in your nervous system. When you sit down and meditate, your mind is clearer, your nervous system is more relaxed and you have a much greater perspective about the day. Rather than being focused on the things you are going to get done, you have a broader perspective like, "I want to make sure I spend time on X" or "It's really important for me to make sure I do something for myself today."

    Then, your to-do list will be reduced to the 3 to 5 most important items. You can then focus on accomplishing those 3 to 5 important items and the other items usually get done without you having to think about them.

There's no need to be thinking about each specific thing you have to accomplish. We have a great ability to do a lot of things without having to think about them. It feels great when you free your mind to be more focused on fewer things.

- *"Can I meditate lying down?"*

I advise against trying to meditate lying down. When you are lying down you are much more likely to have lots of thoughts or fall to sleep.

- *"What can I do if I wake in the middle of the night and I have a hard time going back to sleep?"*

Taking ten deep breaths is very helpful for getting back to sleep if you wake in the middle of the night. As you breathe, let your mind focus on your breath as it moves in and out of your belly. You can extend it to 20, 30 or 50 breaths if necessary. If at the end of that period your mind is still busy, try getting up and meditating for ten minutes. If your mind is still busy after that, extend your meditation for 10 more minutes. Sometimes I have to meditate twice as long as I normally do, then I find I'm yawning and ready to go back to sleep.

Sometimes I get great inspiration in the middle of the night. It is usually during a time when my days are so busy I don't have time to focus on some things that I'd really like to--then I find that I'm up at 3 or 4 am. If after I've tried breathing and meditating, I'm still wide awake I'll leave my bedroom and begin the work that I'm inspired to do. Usually it's some of my best work! Rather than being upset at being up, I just think, "Well, this is a great opportunity to work on this project" and then my next night's sleep is really good.

Mike's Story

I'd like to end this meditation section with an inspirational story about a man I met on the bleachers at my son's football camp. It illustrates that anyone can gain great benefits from meditation. I think it shatters the myths about who meditates and that meditation is only for certain people.

Some people think only yogis, buddhists or strange people meditate. Here's what is really going on... truck drivers, business owners, entrepreneurs, professional athletes, teachers, doctors, nurses, leaders of Fortune 50 corporations and furniture restorers are meditating. People in 3-piece business suits, military uniforms, lab coats, scrubs and prison uniforms are all meditating. You cannot tell who is meditating by what they look like, but you can often tell by their presence and how much you like being around them.

People everywhere are changing their lives for the better. Here is the story of a part-time youth football coach and former construction business owner who now is a happily employed truck driver. Meet Mike...

Mike's stress levels hit an all-time high when his construction business began to crumble due to the changing housing market and the poor economy. He had always felt great about being able to provide his employees with a good livelihood, knowing they could afford nutritious meals for their families and have extra money for presents at Christmas. He often provided lunch for his employees because they worked so hard. In fact, as his business struggled, he found he was more concerned about his employees' well-being than his own.

While Mike had previously lost weight, as the stress of his business increased, so did his weight. He was layering on the pounds he had earlier worked so hard to lose. He felt tired and unhappy. Old injuries to his shoulder and hip were aggravated and painful; he spent a lot of time on the couch.

After the painful laying off of trusted employees and closing of his business, Mike knew he needed to do something to manage his stress. He realized he was carrying a burden so heavy that it was ruining his health and straining his relationships. He knew his weight gain was related to stress and he was tired of feeling exhausted and in pain.

Mike turned to meditation to reduce his stress. He began meditating on his own by making up his own technique. He slowly and deeply breathes while envisioning his stress being squeezed out of his body, much like a tooth paste squeezer pushes toothpaste out of a tube. He imagines his stress being squeezed out of his body from the top of his head, down through his body and out his fingers and toes. He now says he can feel a tingling in his hands when the stress is being released.

This simple meditation practice prompted a chain of powerful changes in Mike's life. As he continued his daily meditation, his sleep improved, he lost weight, and he became excited to exercise and find more ways to get his body moving. He no longer experiences pain in his hip and shoulder, he began eating healthier food, he was more aware of how he is acting in his life and is able to solve family problems in a healthy way.

Mike uses this meditation practice to fall asleep at night. As he lies in bed he imagines the thoughts and stress about everything he has to do the next day, being squeezed out of his mind and down through his body. He now goes to sleep much more quickly and sleeps through the night. If he has to get up to go to the bathroom, he can get right back to sleep.

He also uses his practice to support him during the day. Whenever Mike feels stressed during the day, he takes a few deep breaths and imagines the stress being squeezed out.

The first exercise his meditation practice prompted was stretching. After stretching his body feels much better. He holds each stretch for at least a minute, while breathing slowly and deeply, so his body can gain the full benefit of the stretch. His stretching then lead to walking. Soon after that he began power walking because he had so much more energy and his hip was no longer sore. Then he sought out hilly terrain for long walks. His body felt better than it had in years.

Six months after beginning his meditation practice he is 40 pounds thinner, he has lost over 6 " of belly fat, his diabetes measurement has greatly improved, his triglycerides (the amount of fat in his blood) are less than half and he feels terrific.

Mike feels he owes his gradual and healthy weight loss to meditation--as his practice calms his body and reduces stress hormone levels his metabolism increases and burns more calories. He also feels he wouldn't have sought out a healthier way of eating had he not begun to feel better with meditation, stretching and walking.

After reading an article about how the additives and preservatives in food cause deficiencies and imbalances that lead to water retention and extra weight, Mike began cooking more of his families' meals using fresh foods. His son comments that Mike has become a great cook, because meals taste so much better cooked simply and with healthy ingredients.

Now Mike is inspired to continue to become healthier each day. He is looking forward to being at and sustaining a weight that feels great and continue his learning of healthy habits and exercise. He said, "Meditation has opened my eyes. Now I want to continue growing and learning in new ways to improve the quality of my life and to help my family.

Now that I've started, I'm not stopping! I feel really driven to find even more ways to make my life healthier."

As Mike told me the next part of his story, his emotions showed how much he loves his son. As meditation opened his eyes, he realized he needed to take some action to help his son achieve his dreams of playing football at a Division 1 college. His son's grades weren't what they needed to be to get the football scholarship of his dreams, so he enrolled his son in a six-month Sylvan Learning program. Over this period, his 17 year old son went from a 7th grade reading level to catch up to his grade level. His grades improved significantly, he is more confident in school and he is moving closer to his dream.

Mike is clear that it is time to be helpful to his son without being domineering. He offers his son suggestions, but lets him make his own decisions, knowing they might not be the choices he would make, but that it's time for his son to begin taking ownership for his own decisions.

I keep thinking about how much Mike's eyes sparkled and how strong his voice was when he told me that meditation has turned his life around. His practice is self-taught, quite simple and very powerful. The many improvements in his life are proof it works. Like Mike, anyone with a little self-motivation, can use simple breathing techniques to feel great, improve health and make life more rewarding.

This is what Mike said to me, "I have not felt this good since 1990. I'm loving my new way of life and health. I have so much more energy and a new zest for life. I want to inspire others to grab a hold of life and live it the way it was meant to be lived; full of energy, vitality and vigor!"

Appendix B: Breathing and Meditation Practice Logs

Throughout the five weeks of this program you completed homework each week. This kept you on track practicing the techniques. I don't want to leave you stranded now. At this point you need a tool for making this practice into a strong habit.

One of the best ways to make any change stick is to keep a log. People who use food logs lose more weight. Those who use exercise logs end up becoming more fit and committing to their exercise routine.

Here is a practice log for your breathing or meditation practice to keep yourself on track.

Keep this log next to the place you do your breathing or meditation practice and make a few quick notes when you are done each day. Periodically look back over your log to see your progress and results.

The next few pages contain these logs. You can begin by taking notes in this book, then print additional copies by going to ConsciousSuccess.net/book. I recommend recording your practice in a log for at least the next six months.

Here is a log entry:

Date:_____

Type of practice:

____ Breathing (10 deep breaths)

____ Meditation (5 or more minutes of breathing)

Number of Minutes: _____

Insight I gained during my practice:

_____

_____

Breathing and Meditation Practice Log

Date:_____

Type of practice:

____ Breathing (10 deep breaths)

____ Meditation (5 or more minutes of breathing)

   Number of Minutes: _____

Insight I gained during my practice:

_____

_____

~~~~~~

Date:_____

Type of practice:

____ Breathing (10 deep breaths)

____ Meditation (5 or more minutes of breathing)

   Number of Minutes: _____

Insight I gained during my practice:

_____

_____

~~~~~~

Date:_____

Type of practice:

____ Breathing (10 deep breaths)

____ Meditation (5 or more minutes of breathing)

   Number of Minutes: _____

Insight I gained during my practice:

_____

_____

Breathing and Meditation Practice Log

Date:_____

Type of practice:

____ Breathing (10 deep breaths)

____ Meditation (5 or more minutes of breathing)

    Number of Minutes: _____

Insight I gained during my practice:

_____

_____

~~~~~~~~~~~~~~~~~~~~~~~~~~~~~~~~~~~~~~

Date:_____

Type of practice:

____ Breathing (10 deep breaths)

____ Meditation (5 or more minutes of breathing)

    Number of Minutes: _____

Insight I gained during my practice:

_____

_____

~~~~~~~~~~~~~~~~~~~~~~~~~~~~~~~~~~~~~~

Date:_____

Type of practice:

____ Breathing (10 deep breaths)

____ Meditation (5 or more minutes of breathing)

    Number of Minutes: _____

Insight I gained during my practice:

_____

_____

Breathing and Meditation Practice Log

Date:_____

Type of practice:

____ Breathing (10 deep breaths)

____ Meditation (5 or more minutes of breathing)

Number of Minutes: _____

Insight I gained during my practice:

_____

_____

~~~~~~~~~~~~~~~~~~~~~~~~~~~~~~~~~~~~~

Date:_____

Type of practice:

____ Breathing (10 deep breaths)

____ Meditation (5 or more minutes of breathing)

Number of Minutes: _____

Insight I gained during my practice:

_____

_____

~~~~~~~~~~~~~~~~~~~~~~~~~~~~~~~~~~~~~

Date:_____

Type of practice:

____ Breathing (10 deep breaths)

____ Meditation (5 or more minutes of breathing)

Number of Minutes: _____

Insight I gained during my practice:

_____

_____

Breathing and Meditation Practice Log

Date:_____

Type of practice:

____ Breathing (10 deep breaths)

____ Meditation (5 or more minutes of breathing)

  Number of Minutes: _____

Insight I gained during my practice:

_____

_____

~~~~~~

Date:_____

Type of practice:

____ Breathing (10 deep breaths)

____ Meditation (5 or more minutes of breathing)

  Number of Minutes: _____

Insight I gained during my practice:

_____

_____

~~~~~~

Date:_____

Type of practice:

____ Breathing (10 deep breaths)

____ Meditation (5 or more minutes of breathing)

  Number of Minutes: _____

Insight I gained during my practice:

_____

_____

Breathing and Meditation Practice Log

Date:_____

Type of practice:

____ Breathing (10 deep breaths)

____ Meditation (5 or more minutes of breathing)

Number of Minutes: _____

Insight I gained during my practice:

_____

_____

~~~~~~

Date:_____

Type of practice:

____ Breathing (10 deep breaths)

____ Meditation (5 or more minutes of breathing)

Number of Minutes: _____

Insight I gained during my practice:

_____

_____

~~~~~~

Date:_____

Type of practice:

____ Breathing (10 deep breaths)

____ Meditation (5 or more minutes of breathing)

Number of Minutes: _____

Insight I gained during my practice:

_____

_____

Breathing and Meditation Practice Log

Date:_____

Type of practice:

____ Breathing (10 deep breaths)

____ Meditation (5 or more minutes of breathing)

Number of Minutes: _____

Insight I gained during my practice:

_____

_____

~~~~~~~~~~~~~~~~~~~~~~~~~~~~~~~~~~~~~~

Date:_____

Type of practice:

____ Breathing (10 deep breaths)

____ Meditation (5 or more minutes of breathing)

Number of Minutes: _____

Insight I gained during my practice:

_____

_____

~~~~~~~~~~~~~~~~~~~~~~~~~~~~~~~~~~~~~~

Date:_____

Type of practice:

____ Breathing (10 deep breaths)

____ Meditation (5 or more minutes of breathing)

Number of Minutes: _____

Insight I gained during my practice:

_____

_____

Breathing and Meditation Practice Log

Date:_____

Type of practice:

____ Breathing (10 deep breaths)

____ Meditation (5 or more minutes of breathing)

    Number of Minutes: _____

Insight I gained during my practice:

_____

_____

~~~~~~~~~~~~~~~~~~~~~~~~~~~~~~~~~~~~~~~

Date:_____

Type of practice:

____ Breathing (10 deep breaths)

____ Meditation (5 or more minutes of breathing)

    Number of Minutes: _____

Insight I gained during my practice:

_____

_____

~~~~~~~~~~~~~~~~~~~~~~~~~~~~~~~~~~~~~~~

Date:_____

Type of practice:

____ Breathing (10 deep breaths)

____ Meditation (5 or more minutes of breathing)

    Number of Minutes: _____

Insight I gained during my practice:

_____

_____

Breathing and Meditation Practice Log

Date:_____

Type of practice:

____ Breathing (10 deep breaths)

____ Meditation (5 or more minutes of breathing)

Number of Minutes: _____

Insight I gained during my practice:

_____

_____

~~~~~~~~~~~~~~~~~~~~~~~~~~~~~~~~~~~~~~

Date:_____

Type of practice:

____ Breathing (10 deep breaths)

____ Meditation (5 or more minutes of breathing)

Number of Minutes: _____

Insight I gained during my practice:

_____

_____

~~~~~~~~~~~~~~~~~~~~~~~~~~~~~~~~~~~~~~

Date:_____

Type of practice:

____ Breathing (10 deep breaths)

____ Meditation (5 or more minutes of breathing)

Number of Minutes: _____

Insight I gained during my practice:

_____

_____

Appendix C: Executive Interviews

While writing this book, I interviewed 11 executives to gain perspective on the challenges facing both employers and employees related to stress, engagement, performance and productivity. Some interviews were with Human Resource professionals and some were with business unit heads. The companies spanned small (a few hundred employees) to large (Fortune 50) organizations.

This is who was interviewed:

Company	Role
New York Life	Senior Vice President, Chief HR Officer
New York Life	Chief Talent Officer
Verizon	Manager
PlumChoice, Inc.	HR Director
Neighborhood Health Plan	Vice President of HR
Large Retail Organization	Senior Vice President, Director of HR
Veolia Energy	Vice President of HR
Genzyme	Director, Leadership & Organizational Development
Willis Group	Executive Vice President
Invesco Ltd.	Managing Director
Global Financial Investment and Advisory Firm	Senior Managing Director

I was impressed by the focus these companies have on increasing engagement and performance within their companies. It is clear the business case for improving morale has been made. These companies see that increased morale is necessary to increasing productivity. They also understand that spending time helping employees to become engaged is the key to enhancing performance and increasing profits.

Organizational stress, which is referred to on page 10, is something highly functioning and emotionally intelligent organizations understand must be minimized for their employees to perform at their highest levels. Organizational stress includes the following: turf protection, being in survival mode and withholding information, distrust, incivility, finger pointing, blame and backstabbing.

Here are some of the ways these companies are increase performance among their employees:

- A global financial investment and advisory firm works hard to keep staff insulated from distractions of high level company politics and regulatory changes. The goal is to keep staff focused on their own goals and then get them involved only as needed in the larger corporate issues.

  ★Employees are rewarded for team work. Incentives are awarded at the team level, so employees work hard to support each other in expanding business and keeping clients satisfied.

- Willis executives work hard to get rid of distractions by having a transparent and flat organization. When they see pockets of organizational stress, they resolve the situations immediately.

★They freeze pay and only pay bonuses for growth when necessary to ensure the health of the organization. They offer additional unpaid days off for those employees who value additional time off.

- Genzyme has always prided itself on being a mission driven company. They have pictures of their actual patients throughout all buildings. Employees see whose lives they are saving and making better on a daily basis. This goes a long way in engaging employees.

- Veolia Energy, a leading operator and developer of efficient energy solutions, has an engaged and dedicated employee base. This could be because the company's commitment to preserving the environment is close to many employees' hearts. Veolia Energy also creates incentives for employees to collaborate, think creatively, and generate ideas to increase environmental sustainability and improve operational performance through an Efficiency Suggestion Program. In addition, to help optimize employee health, Veolia has implemented certain preventative care requirements, and pays 100% of this cost for employees.

- A large retail organization manages stress for their employees by carefully managing the amount of communication which employees receive. Management provides a gatekeeping role by limiting unnecessary communication, saying no when necessary for employees and offering a recognition budget to those employees who are meeting or exceeding their goals.

  ★ This company also spends a substantial amount of time and money on talent development, acquisition and management. They understand their store managers are essential to sustaining the growth they desire. Leadership assessments are used and talent reviews are conducted semi-annually with quarterly updates. They identify high-potential talent and have rich development plans.

- Neighborhood Health Plan has been certified by the American Heart Association for the past three years as a "Heart Healthy" organization. They offer smoking cessation, yoga, zumba, self defense and meditation classes to employees. They also do fun things like a "Take the Stairs" program, charades and other games, and walking contests.

  ★ In order to get groups to work better together and reduce any silo effect, groups have official Service Level Agreements between each other. These agreements explain roles, responsibilities, resources, how quickly they will respond to each other and how communication between the groups is handled. This is a simple and smart way to set expectations and reduce conflict.

- PlumChoice, a company which offers software and services for delivering premium technology support and IT Service Desk automation, helps their employees manage stress by forming a Culture Crew. This cross-departmental team, including the CEO, determines how to increase engagement among employees and create a more fun, interesting, and creative work environment. They have replaced their traditional conference room furnishings with comfortable chairs, small tables and white board walls.

- Verizon's Vendor Relationship Team Manager invited me to work with her team. As a result of our half day session, they increased their ability to communicate with each other, creatively manage projects and impress senior executives with new creative solutions. The team began working together in a more focused way and now accomplish more with fewer resources. Members of the team have since been promoted, including the Manager.

- One of New York Life's missions is to create a distributive leadership culture by empowering managers to make more decisions. They hold an off site training experience called "Leader as Coach" for their top 100 managers. The goal is to help their executives learn how to drill down to the root of a problem more quickly and effectively and then to solve it accurately to increase business results.

  ★ They have a comprehensive coaching and leadership development program and are seriously investing in mid level development programs and diversity.

  ★ New York Life believes that meaningful work drives engagement and they work hard to ensure employees are doing work they find meaningful.

  ★ They also recently redesigned their management performance process to adjust the cadence of manager contact with employees which gives managers the best insight into how employees are really doing.

It is encouraging to see so many companies working hard to make their environments more engaging, collaborative, rewarding and fun places to work.

This is my wish for all companies and employees, all over the globe.

Jacqueline Brodntizki, President, Conscious Success LLC

Jacqueline is a consultant, executive coach, author, speaker and President of Conscious Success LLC. She launched the firm in 2009 to help customer service organizations increase performance, productivity and profits. Conscious Success clients realize significant cost savings due to dramatically reduced attrition, absenteeism and medical care claims. Clients' employees are less stressed, more engaged and stay employed longer.

Jacqueline combines over 15 years of corporate management and training expertise with nine years of teaching and coaching of mindfulness and stress reduction techniques to help companies reduce employee stress and increase performance, productivity, and profits.

Earlier in her career, she spent over 15 years working with Fortune 100 Companies while employed by Hewitt and New York Life Retirement Plan Services (NYLIM). She served as a Trainer, Consultant, held various management roles and was Vice President of Client Services where she created the relationship management function to manage the overall relationship for NYLIM's Retirement Plan clients.

Her staff of Relationship Managers, who handled over 200 client relationships across the United States coordinating a broad range of services, consistently received the highest client satisfaction ratings on third party surveys.

Jacqueline is accredited by the Hay Group to consult with companies based on the Emotional and Social Intelligence Competency Instrument.

She is also the author of the book, *Awaken Your Inner Radiance* and the CDs: *Inner Balance*

Meditation CD and *Inner Balance Yoga CD*. The books and CDs are available on Amazon.

She is a guest blogger for NorthEast Human Resources Association (NEHRA) and ContactCenterWorld.com, speaks at various conferences and events, and presents on webcasts for NEHRA and HR.com.

Jacqueline is a member of:

• Human Resources Leadership Forum

• Northeast Human Resources Association

• NEHRA Learning and Organizational Development Forum

• The Commonwealth Institute

• ContactCenterWorld

Jacqueline can be reached at:

www.ConsciousSuccess.net

Jacqueline@ConsciousSuccess.net

1-800-270-6722

Visit ConsciousSuccess.net/book for these valuable items:

• Printable practice logs

• Recordings of the breathing and meditation exercises in this book

• As our thanks for purchasing this book, receive a 66% discount on our Conscious Success Virtual Course. Click on the link for the course on the web page and enter the discount code 'book' when you check out.

Made in the USA
Lexington, KY
23 April 2012